PREFACE

The success of her little book entitled "Seventy-five Receipts in Cakes, Pastry, and Sweetmeats." has encouraged the author to attempt a larger and more miscellaneous work on the subject of cookery, comprising as far as practicable whatever is most useful in its various departments; and particularly adapted to the domestic economy of her own country. Designing it as a manual of American housewifery, she has avoided the insertion of any dishes whose ingredients cannot be procured on our side of the Atlantic, and which require for their preparation utensils that are rarely found except in Europe. Also, she has omitted every thing which may not, by the generality of tastes, be considered good of its kind, and well worth the trouble and cost of preparing.

The author has spared no pains in collecting and arranging, perhaps the greatest number of practical and original receipts that have ever appeared in a similar work; flattering herself that she has rendered them so explicit as to be easily understood, and followed, even by inexperienced cooks. The directions are given as minutely as if each receipt was "to stand alone by itself," all references to others being avoided; except in some few instances to the one immediately preceding; it being a just cause of complaint that in some of the late cookery books, the reader, before finishing the article, is desired to search out pages and numbers in remote parts of the volume.

In the hope that her system of cookery may be consulted with equal advantage by families in town and in country, by those whose condition makes it expedient to practise economy, and by others whose circumstances authorize a liberal expenditure, the author sends it to take its chance among the multitude of similar publications, satisfied that it will meet with as much success as it may be found to deserve,—more she has no right to expect.

Philadelphia, April 15th, 1837.

INTRODUCTORY HINTS.

WEIGHTS AND MEASURES.

We recommend to all families that they should keep in the house: a pair of scales, (one of the scales deep enough to hold flour, sugar, &c., conveniently,) and a set of tin measures: as accuracy in proportioning the ingredients is indispensable to success in cookery. It is best to have the scales permanently fixed to a small beam projecting (for instance) from one of the shelves of the store-room. This will preclude the frequent inconvenience of their getting twisted, unlinked, and otherwise out of order; a common consequence of putting them in and out of their box, and carrying them from place to place. The weights (of which there should be a set from two pounds to a quarter of an ounce) ought carefully to be kept in the box, that none of them may be lost or mislaid.

A set of tin measures (with small spouts or lips) from a gallon down to half a jill, will be found very convenient in every kitchen; though common pitchers, bowls, glasses, &c. may be substituted. It is also well to have a set of wooden measures from a bushel to a quarter of a peck.

Let it be remembered, that of liquid measure—

- Two jills are half a pint.
- Two pints—one quart.
- Four quarts—one gallon.

Of dry measure—

- Half a gallon is a quarter of a peck.

- One gallon—half a peck.
- Two gallons—one peck.
- Four gallons—half a bushel.
- Eight gallons—one bushel.

About twenty-five drops of any thin liquid will fill a common sized tea-spoon.

Four table-spoonfuls or half a jill, will fill a common wine glass.

Four wine glasses will fill a half-pint or common tumbler, or a large coffee-cup.

A quart black bottle holds in reality about a pint and a half.

Of flour, butter, sugar, and most articles used in cakes and pastry, a quart is generally about equal in quantity to a pound avoirdupois, (sixteen ounces.) Avoirdupois is the weight designated throughout this book.

Ten eggs generally weigh one pound before they are broken.

A table-spoonful of salt is generally about one ounce.

SOUPS.

GENERAL REMARKS.

Always use soft water for making soup, and be careful to proportion the quantity of water to that of the meat. Somewhat less than a quart of water to a pound of meat, is a good rule for common soups. Rich soups, intended for company, may have a still smaller allowance of water.

Soup should always be made entirely of fresh meat that has not been previously cooked. An exception to this rule may sometimes be made in favour of the remains of a piece of roast beef that has been *very much* under-done in roasting. This may be *added* to a good piece of raw meat. Cold ham, also, may be occasionally put into white soups.

Soup made of cold meat has always a vapid, disagreeable taste, very perceptible through all the seasoning, and which nothing indeed can disguise. Also, it will be of a bad, dingy colour. The juices of the meat having been exhausted by the first cooking, the undue proportion of watery liquid renders it, for soup, indigestible and unwholesome, as well as unpalatable. As there is little or no nutriment to be derived from soup made with cold meat, it is better to refrain from using it for this purpose, and to devote the leavings of the table to some other object. No person accustomed to really good soup, made from fresh meat, can ever be deceived in the taste, even when flavoured with wine and spices. It is not true that French cooks have the art of producing *excellent* soups from cold scraps. There is much *bad* soup to be found in France, at inferior houses; but *good* French cooks are not, as is generally supposed, really in the practice of concocting any dishes out of the refuse of the table. And we repeat, that cold meat, even when perfectly good, and used in a large quantity, has not sufficient substance to flavour soup, or to render it wholesome.

Soup, however, that has been originally made of raw meat entirely, is frequently better the second day than the first; provided that it is re-boiled only for a very short time, and that no additional water is added to it.

Unless it has been allowed to boil too hard, so as to exhaust the water, the soup-pot will not require replenishing. When it is found absolutely necessary to do so, the additional water must be boiling hot when poured in; if lukewarm or cold, it will entirely spoil the soup.

Every particle of fat should be carefully skimmed from the surface. Greasy soup is disgusting and unwholesome. The lean of meat is much better for soup than the fat.

Long and slow boiling is necessary to extract the strength from the meat. If boiled fast over a large fire, the meat becomes hard and tough, and will not give out its juices.

Potatoes, if boiled in the soup, are thought by some to render it unwholesome, from the opinion that the water in which potatoes have been cooked is almost a poison. As potatoes are a part of every dinner, it is very easy to take a few out of the pot in which they have been boiled by themselves, and to cut them up and add them to the soup just before it goes to table.

The cook should season the soup but very slightly with salt and pepper. If she puts in too much, it may spoil it for the taste of most of those that are to eat it; but if too little, it is easy to add more to your own plate.

The practice of thickening soup by stirring flour into it is not a good one, as it spoils both the appearance and the taste. If made with a sufficient quantity of good fresh meat, and not too much water, and if boiled long and slowly, it will have substance enough without flour.

FAMILY SOUP.

Take a shin or leg of beef that has been newly killed; the fore leg is best, as there is the most meat on it. Have it cut into three pieces, and wash it well. To each pound allow somewhat less than a quart of water; for instance, to ten pounds of leg of beef, nine quarts of water is a good proportion. Put it into a large pot, and add half a table-spoonful of salt. Hang it over a good fire, as early as six o'clock in the morning, if you dine at two. When it has come to a hard boil, and the scum has risen, (which it will do as soon as it has boiled,) skim it well. Do not remove the lid more frequently than is absolutely necessary, as uncovering the pot causes the flavour to evaporate. Then set it on hot coals in the corner, and keep it simmering steadily, adding fresh coals so as to continue a regular heat.

About nine o'clock, put in four carrots, one parsnip, and a large onion cut into slices, and four small turnips, and eight tomatas, also cut up; add a head of celery cut small. Put in a very small head of cabbage, cut into little pieces. If you have any objection to cabbage, substitute a larger proportion of the other vegetables. Put in also a bunch of sweet marjoram, tied up in a thin muslin rag to prevent its floating on the top.

Let the soup simmer unceasingly till two o'clock, skimming it well: then take it up, and put it into a tureen. If your dinner hour is later, you may of course begin the soup later; but it will require at least eight hours' cooking; remembering to put in the vegetables three hours after the meat.

If you wish to send the meat to table, take the best part of it out of the soup, about two hours before dinner. Have ready another pot with a dozen tomatas and a few cloves. Moisten them with a little of the soup, just sufficient to keep them from burning. When the tomatas have stewed down soft, put the meat upon them, and let it brown till dinner time over a few coals, keeping the pot closely covered; then send it to table on a dish by itself. Let the remainder of the meat be left in the large pot till you send up the soup, as by that time it will be boiled to rags and have transferred all its flavour to the liquid.

This soup will be greatly improved by the addition of a few dozen ochras cut into very thin slices, and put in with the other vegetables. You may put Lima beans into it, green peas, or indeed any vegetables you like: or you may thicken it with ochras and tomatas only.

Next day, take what is left of the soup, put it into a pot, and simmer it over hot coals for half an hour: a longer time will weaken the taste. If it has been well made and kept in a cool place, it will be found better the second day than the first.

If your family is very small, and the leg of beef large, and the season winter, it may furnish soup for four successive days. Cut the beef in half; make soup of the first half, in the manner above directed, and have the remainder warmed next day; then on the third day make fresh soup of the second half.

We have been minute in these directions; for if strictly followed, the soup, though plain, will be found excellent.

If you do not intend to serve up the meat separately, break to pieces all the bones with a mallet or kitchen cleaver. This, by causing them to give out their marrow, &c., will greatly enrich the liquid. Do this, of course, when you first begin the soup.

FINE BEEF SOUP.

Begin this soup the day before it is wanted. Take a good piece of fresh beef that has been newly killed: any substantial part will do that has not too much fat about it: a fore leg is very good for this purpose. Wash it well. Cut off all the meat, and break up the bones. Put the meat and the bones into a large pot, very early in the day, so as to allow eight or nine hours for its boiling. Proportion the water to the quantity of meat—about a pint and a half to each pound. Sprinkle the meat with a small quantity of pepper and salt. Pour on the water, hang it over a moderate fire, and boil it slowly; carefully skimming off all the fat that rises to the top, and keeping it closely covered, except when you raise the lid to skim it. Do not, on any account, put in additional water to this soup while it is boiling; and take care that the boiling goes steadily on, as, if it stops, the soup will be much injured. But if the fire is too great, and the soup boils too fast, the meat will become hard and tough, and will not give out its juices.

After the meat is reduced to rags, and the soup sufficiently boiled, remove the pot from the fire, and let it stand in the corner for a quarter of an hour to settle. Then take it up, strain it into a large earthen pan, cover it, and set it away in a cool dry place till next day. Straining it makes it clear and bright, and frees it from the shreds of meat and bone. If you find that it jellies in the pan, (which it will if properly made,) do not disturb it till you are ready to put it into the pot for the second boiling, as breaking the jelly may prevent it from keeping well.

On the following morning, boil separately, carrots, turnips, onions, celery, and whatever other vegetables you intend to thicken the soup with. Tomatas will greatly improve it. Prepare them by taking off the skin, cutting them into small pieces, and stewing them in their own juice till they are entirely dissolved. Put on the carrots before any of the other vegetables, as they require the longest time to boil. Or you may slice and put into the soup a portion of the vegetables you are boiling for dinner; but they must be nearly done before you put them in, as the second boiling of the soup should not exceed half an hour, or indeed, just sufficient time to heat it thoroughly.

Scrape off carefully from the cake of jellied soup whatever fat or sediment may still be remaining on it; divide the jelly into pieces, and about half an hour before it is to go to table, put it into a pot, add the various vegetables, (having first sliced them,) in sufficient quantities to make the soup very thick; hang it over the fire and let it boil slowly, or simmer steadily till dinner time. Boiling it much on the second day will destroy the flavour, and render it flat and insipid. For this reason, in making fine, clear beef soup, the vegetables are to be cooked separately. They need not be put in the first day, as the soup is to be strained; and on the second day, if put in raw, the length of time required to cook them would spoil the soup by doing it too much. We repeat, that when soup has been sufficiently boiled on the first day, and all the juices and flavour of the meat thoroughly extracted, half an hour is the utmost it requires on the second.

Carefully avoid seasoning it too highly. Soup, otherwise excellent, is frequently spoiled by too much pepper and salt. These condiments can be added at table, according to the taste of those that are eating it; but if too large a proportion of them is put in by the cook, there is then no remedy, and the soup may by some be found uneatable.

Many persons prefer boiling all the vegetables in the soup on the first day, thinking that they improve its flavour. This may be done in common soup that is not to be strained, but is inadmissible if you wish it to be very bright and clear. Also, unless you have a garden and a profusion of vegetables of your own, it is somewhat extravagant, as when strained out they are of no further use, and are therefore wasted.

MUTTON SOUP.

Cut off the shoulder part of a fore quarter of mutton, and having cut all the meat from the bone, put it into a soup pot with two quarts of water. As soon as it boils, skim it well, and then slacken the fire and simmer the meat for an hour and a half. Then take the remainder of the mutton, and put it whole into the soup-pot with sufficient boiling water to cover it well, and salt it to your taste. Skim it the moment the fresh piece of meat begins to boil, and about every quarter of an hour afterwards. It should boil slowly five hours. Prepare half a dozen turnips, four carrots, and three onions, (all cut up, but not small,) and put them in about an hour and a half before dinner. [Footnote: The carrots should be put in early, as they require a long time to boil; if full grown, at least three hours.] You may also put in some small dumplings. Add some chopped parsley.

Cut the meat off the scrag into small pieces, and send it to table in the tureen with the soup. The other half of the mutton should be served on a separate dish, with whole turnips boiled and laid round it. Many persons are fond of mutton that has been boiled in soup.

You may thicken this soup with rice or barley that has first been soaked in cold water; or with green peas; or with young corn, cut down from the cob; or with tomatas scalded, peeled, and cut into pieces.

Cabbage Soup may be made in the same manner, of neck of mutton. Omit all the other vegetables, and put in a large head of white cabbage, stripped of the outside leaves, and cut small.

Noodle Soup can be made in this manner also. Noodles are a mixture of flour and beaten egg, made into a stiff paste, kneaded, rolled out very thin, and cut into long narrow slips, not thicker than straws, and then dried three or four hours in the sun, on tin or pewter plates. They must be put in the soup shortly before dinner, as, if boiled too long they will go to pieces.

With the mutton that is taken from the soup you may send to table some suet dumplings, boiled in another pot, and served on a separate dish. Make them in the proportion of half a pound of beef suet to a pound and a quarter of flour. Chop the suet as fine as possible, rub it into the flour, and mix it into a dough with a little cold water. Roll it out thick, and cut it into dumplings about as large as the top of a tumbler, and boil them an hour.

VEAL SOUP.

The knuckle or leg of veal is the best for soup. Wash it and break up the bones. Put it into a pot with a pound of ham or bacon cut into pieces, and water enough to cover the meat. A set of calf's feet, cut in half, will greatly improve it. After it has stewed slowly, till all the meat drops to pieces, strain it, return it to the pot, and put in a head of celery cut small, three onions, a bunch of sweet marjoram, a carrot and a turnip cut into pieces, and two dozen black pepper-corns, with salt to your taste. Add some small dumplings made of flour and butter. Simmer it another hour, or till all the vegetables are sufficiently done, and thus send it to table.

You may thicken it with noodles, that is paste made of flour and beaten egg, and cut into long thin slips. Or with vermicelli, rice, or barley; or with green peas, or asparagus tops.

RICH VEAL SOUP.

Take three pounds of the scrag of a neck of veal, cut it into pieces, and put it with the bones (which must be broken up) into a pot with two quarts of water. Stew it till the meat is done to rags, and skim it well. Then strain it and return it to the pot.

Blanch and pound in a mortar to a smooth paste, a quarter of a pound of sweet almonds, and mix them with the yolks of six hard boiled eggs grated, mid a pint of cream, which must first have been boiled or it will curdle in the soup. Season it with nutmeg and mace. Stir the mixture into the soup, and let it boil afterward about three minutes, stirring all the time. Lay in the bottom of the tureen some slices of bread without the crust. Pour the soup upon it, and send it to table.

CLEAR GRAVY SOUP.

Having well buttered the inside of a nicely tinned stew-pot, cut half a pound of ham into slices, and lay them at the bottom, with three pounds of the lean of fresh beef, and as much veal, cut from the bones, which you must afterward break to pieces, and lay on the meat. Cover the pan closely, and set it over a quick fire. When the meat begins to stick to the pan, turn it; and when there is a nice brown glaze at the bottom, cover the meat with cold water. Watch it well, and when it is just coming to a boil, put in half a pint of cold water. This will cause the scum to rise. Skim it well, and then pour in another half pint of cold water; skim it again; pour in cold water as before, half a pint at a time, and repeat this till no more scum rises. In skimming, carefully avoid stirring the soup, as that will injure its clearness.

In the mean time prepare your vegetables. Peel off the outer skin of three large white onions and slice them. Pare three large turnips, and slice them also. Wash clean and cut into small pieces three carrots, and three large heads of celery. If you cannot obtain fresh celery, substitute a large table-spoonful of celery seed, tied up in a bit of clear muslin. Put the vegetables into the soup, and then place the pot on one side of the fire, where the heat is not so great as in the middle. Let it boil gently for four hours. Then strain the soup through a fine towel or linen bag into a large stone pan, but do not squeeze the bag, or the soup will be cloudy, and look dull instead of clear. In pouring it into the straining cloth, be careful not to disturb the ingredients at the bottom of the soup-pot.

This soup should be of a fine clear amber colour. If not perfectly bright after straining, you may clarify it in this manner. Put it into the stew-pan. Break the whites of two eggs into a basin, carefully avoiding the smallest particle of the yolk. Beat the white of egg to a stiff froth, and then mix it gradually with the soup. Set it over the fire, and stir it till it boils briskly. Then take it off, and set it beside the fire to settle for ten minutes. Strain it then through a clean napkin, and it will be fit for use. But it is better to have the soup clear by making it carefully, than to depend on clarifying it afterward, as the white of egg weakens the taste.

In making this (which is quite a show-soup) it is customary to reverse the general rule, and pour in cold water.

SOUPE À LA JULIENNE.

Make a gravy soup as in the preceding receipt, and strain it before you put in the vegetables. Cut some turnips and carrots into ribands, and some onions and celery into lozenges or long diamond-shaped pieces. Boil them separately. When the vegetables are thoroughly boiled, put them with the soup into the tureen, and then lay gently on the top some small squares of toasted bread without crust; taking care that they do not crumble down and disturb the brightness of the soup, which should be of a clear amber colour.

MACCARONI SOUP.

This also is made of clear gravy soup. Cut up and boil the maccaroni by itself in a very little water, allowing a quarter of a pound to a quart of soup. The pieces should be about an inch long. Put a small piece of butter with it. It must boil till tender, but not till it breaks. Throw it into the soup shortly before it goes to table, and give it one boil up. Send to table with it a plate or glass of rasped Parmesan or other rich cheese, with a dessert spoon in it, that those who like it may put it into their soup on the plate.

While the maccaroni is boiling, take care that it does not get into lumps.

RICH MACCARONI SOUP.

Take a quart of clear gravy soup, and boil in it a pound of the best maccaroni cut into pieces. When it is tender, take out half of the maccaroni, and add to the remainder two quarts more of the soup. Boil it till the maccaroni is entirely dissolved and incorporated with the liquid. Strain it; then return it to the soup-pan, and add to it the remainder of the maccaroni, (that was taken out before the pieces broke,) and put in a quarter of a pound of grated Parmesan cheese. Let it simmer awhile, but take it up before it comes to a boil.

It may be made with milk instead of gravy soup.

VERMICELLI SOUP.

Cut a knuckle of veal, or a neck of mutton into small pieces, and put them, with the bones broken up, into a large stew-pan. Add the meat sliced from a hock or shank of ham, a quarter of a pound of butter, two large onions sliced, a bunch of sweet herbs, and a head of celery cut small. Cover the pan closely, and set it without any water over a slow fire for an hour or more, to extract the essence from the meat. Then skim it well, and pour in four quarts of boiling water, and let it boil gently till all the meat is reduced to rags. Strain it, set it again on the fire, and add a quarter of a pound of vermicelli, which has first been scalded in boiling water. Season it to your taste with salt and cayenne pepper, and let it boil five minutes. Lay a large slice of bread in the bottom of your tureen, and pour the soup upon it.

For the veal or mutton you may substitute a pair of large fowls cut into pieces; always adding the ham or a few slices of bacon, without which it will be insipid. Old fowls that are fit for no other purpose will do very well for soup.

MILK SOUP.

Boil two quarts of milk with a quarter of a pound of sweet almonds, and two ounces of bitter ones, blanched and broken to pieces, and a large stick of cinnamon broken up. Stir in sugar enough to make it very sweet. When it has boiled strain it. Cut some thin slices of bread, and (having pared off the crust) toast them. Lay them in the bottom of a tureen, pour a little of the hot milk over them, and cover them close, that they may soak. Beat the yolks of five eggs very light Set the milk on hot coals, and add the eggs to it by degrees; stirring it all the time till it thickens. Then take it off instantly, lest it curdle, and pour it into the tureen, boiling hot, over the bread.

This will be still better if you cover the bottom with slices of baked apple.

RICH BROWN SOUP.

Take six pounds of the lean of fresh beef, cut from the bone. Stick it over with four dozen cloves. Season it with a tea-spoonful of salt, a tea-spoonful of pepper, a tea-spoonful of mace, and a beaten nutmeg. Slice half a dozen onions; fry them in butter; chop them, and spread them over the meat after you have put it into the soup-pot. Pour in five quarts of water, and stew it slowly for five or six hours; skimming it well. When the meat has dissolved into shreds, strain it, and return the liquid to the pot. Then add a tumbler and a half, or six wine glasses of claret or port wine. Simmer it again slowly till dinner time. When the soup is reduced to three quarts, it is done enough. Put it into a tureen, and send it to table.

RICH WHITE SOUP.

Take a pair of large fat fowls. Cut them up. Butter the inside of the soup-pot, and put in the pieces of fowl with two pounds of the lean of veal, cut into pieces, or with four calf's feet cut in half. Season them with a tea-spoonful of salt, a half tea-spoonful of cayenne pepper, and a dozen blades of mace. Cover them with water, and stew it slowly for an hour, skimming it well. Then take out the breasts and wings of the fowls, and having cut off the flesh, chop it fine. Keep the pot covered, and the veal and the remainder of the fowls still stewing.

Mix the chopped chicken with the grated crumb of about one quarter of a loaf of stale bread, (a six cent loaf,) having soaked the crumbs in a little warm milk. Have ready the yolks of four hard boiled eggs, a dozen sweet almonds, and half a dozen bitter ones blanched and broken small. Mix the egg and almonds with the chopped chicken and grated bread, and pound all in a mortar till it is well incorporated. Strain the soup from the meat and fowl, and stir this mixture into the liquid, after it has stewed till reduced to two quarts. Having boiled separately a quart of cream or rich milk, add it hot to the soup, a little at a time. Cover it, and let it simmer a few minutes longer. Then send it to table.

These two soups (the brown and the white) are suited to dinner parties.

MEG MERRILIES' SOUP.

Take four pounds of venison, or if you cannot procure venison you may substitute the lean of fresh beef or mutton. Season it with pepper and salt, put it into a large pot, (break the bones and lay them on the meat,) pour in four quarts of water, and boil it three hours, skimming it well. Then strain it, and put it into another pot.

Cut up a hare or a rabbit, a pair of partridges, and a pair of grouse; or one of each, with a pheasant, a woodcock, or any other game that you can most easily obtain. Season them and put them into the soup. Add a dozen small onions, a couple of heads of celery cut small, and half a dozen sliced potatoes. Let the soup simmer till the game is sufficiently done, and all the vegetables tender.

This is the soup with which the gipsy, Meg Merrilies, regaled Dominie Sampson.

When game is used for soup, it must be newly killed, and quite fresh.

VENISON SOUP.

Take four pounds of freshly killed venison cut off from the bones, and one pound of ham in small slices. Add an onion minced, and black pepper to your taste. Put only as much water as will cover it, and stew it gently for an hour, keeping the pot closely covered. Then skim it well, and pour in a quart of boiling water. Add a head of celery cut into small pieces, and half a dozen blades of mace. Boil it gently two hours and a half. Then put in a quarter of a pound of butter, divided into small pieces and rolled in flour, and half a pint of port or Madeira wine. Let it boil a quarter of an hour longer, and then send it to table with the meat in it.

HARE OR RABBIT SOUP.

Take a large newly killed hare, or two rabbits; cut them up and wash the pieces. Save all the blood, (which adds much to the flavour of the hare,) and strain it through a sieve. Put the pieces into a soup-pot with four whole onions stuck with a few cloves, four or five blades of mace, a head of celery cut small, and a bunch of parsley with a large sprig of sweet marjoram and one of sweet basil, all tied together. Salt and cayenne to your taste. Pour in three quarts of water, and stew it gently an hour and a half. Then put in the strained blood and simmer it for another hour, at least. Do not let it actually boil, as that will cause the blood to curdle. Then strain it, and pound half the meat in a mortar, and stir it into the soup to thicken it, and cut the remainder of the meat into small mouthfuls. Stir in, at the last, a jill or two glasses of red wine, and a large table-spoonful of currant jelly. Boil it slowly a few minutes longer, and then put it into your tureen. It will be much improved by the addition of about a dozen and a half small force-meat balls, about the size of a nutmeg. This soup will require cooking at least four hours.

Partridge, pheasant, or grouse soup may be made in a similar manner.

If you have any clear gravy soup, you may cut up the hare, season it as above, and put it into a jug or jar well covered, and set in boiling water till the meat is tender. Then put it into the gravy soup, add the wine, and let it come to a boil. Send it to table with the pieces of the hare in the soup.

When hare soup is made in this last manner, omit using the blood.

MULLAGATAWNY SOUP, AS MADE IN INDIA.

Take a quarter of an ounce of China turmeric, the third of an ounce of cassia, three drachms of black pepper, two drachms of cayenne pepper, and an ounce of coriander seeds. These must all be pounded fine in a mortar, and well mixed and sifted. They will make sufficient curry powder for the following quantity of soup:

Take two large fowls, or three pounds of the lean of veal. Cut the flesh entirely from the bones in small pieces, and put it into a stew-pan with two quarts of water. Let it boil slowly for half an hour, skimming it well.

Prepare four large onions, minced and fried in two ounces of butter. Add to them the curry powder and moisten the whole with broth from the stew-pan, mixed with a little rice flour. When thoroughly mixed, stir the seasoning into the soup, and simmer it till it is as smooth and thick as cream, and till the chicken or veal is perfectly tender. Then stir into it the juice of a lemon; and five minutes after take up the soup, with the meat in it, and serve it in the tureen.

Send to table separately, boiled rice on a hot-water dish to keep it warm, The rice is to be put into the plates of soup by those who eat it.

To boil rice for this soup in the East India fashion:—Pick and wash half a pound in warm water. Put it into a sauce-pan. Pour two quarts of boiling water over it, and cover the pan closely. Set it in a warm place by the fire, to cook gradually in the hot water. In an hour pour off all the water, and setting the pan on hot coals, stir up and toss the rice with a fork, so as to separate the grains, and to dry without hardening it. Do not use a spoon, as that will not loosen the grains sufficiently.

MOCK TURTLE OR CALF'S HEAD SOUP.

This soup will require eight hours to prepare. Take a large calf's head, and having cleaned, washed, and soaked it, put it into a pot with a knuckle of veal, and the hock of a ham, or a few slices of bacon; but previously cut off and reserve enough of the veal to make two dozen small force-meat balls. Put the head and the other meat into as much water as will cover it very well, so that it may not be necessary to replenish it: this soup being always made very rich. Let it boil slowly four hours, skimming it carefully. As soon as no more scum rises, put in six potatoes, and three turnips, all sliced thin; with equal proportions of parsley, sweet marjoram and sweet basil, chopped fine; and pepper and salt to your taste.

An hour before you send the meat to table, make about two dozen small force-meat balls of minced veal and beef-suet in equal quantities, seasoned with pepper and salt; sweet herbs, grated lemon-peel, and powdered nutmeg and mace. Add some beaten yolk of egg to make all these ingredients stick together. Flour the balls very well, and fry them in butter. Before you put them into the soup, take out the head, and the other meat. Cut the meat from the head in small pieces, and return it to the soup. When the soup is nearly done, stir in half a pint of Madeira. Have ready at least a dozen egg-balls made of the yolks of hard-boiled eggs, grated or pounded in a mortar, and mixed with a little flour and sufficient raw yolk of egg to bind them. Make them up into the form and size of boy's marbles. Throw them into the soup at the last, and also squeeze in the juice of a lemon. Let it get another slow boil, and then put it into the tureen.

We omit a receipt for *real* turtle soup, as when that very expensive, complicated, and difficult dish is prepared in a private family, it is advisable to hire a first-rate cook for the express purpose.

An easy way is to get it ready made, in any quantity you please, from a turtle-soup house.

OX TAIL SOUP.

Three ox tails will make a large tureen full of soup. Desire the butcher to divide them at the joints. Rub them with salt, and put them to soak in warm water, while you prepare the vegetables. Put into a large pot or stew-pan four onions peeled and quartered, a bunch of parsley, two sliced carrots, two sliced turnips, and two dozen pepper corns. Then put in the tails, and pour on three quarts of water.

Cover the pot, and set it on hot coals by the side of the fire. Keep it gently simmering for about three hours, supplying it well with fresh hot coals. Skim it carefully. When the meat is quite tender, and falls from the bones, strain the soup into another pot, and add to it a spoonful of mushroom catchup, and two spoonfuls of butter rubbed in flour.

You may thicken it also with the pulp of a dozen onions first fried soft, and then rubbed through a cullender. After it is thickened, let it just boil up, and then send it to table, with small squares of toasted bread in the tureen.

OCHRA SOUP.

Take a large slice of ham (cold boiled ham is best) and two pounds of the lean of fresh beef; cut all the meat into small pieces. Add a quarter of a pound of butter slightly melted; twelve large tomatas pared and cut small; five dozen ochras cut into slices not thicker than a cent; and salt and cayenne pepper to your taste. Put all these ingredients into a pot; cover them with boiling water, and let them stew slowly for an hour. Then add three quarts of *hot* water, and increase the heat so as to make the soup boil. Skim it well, and stir it frequently with a wooden or silver spoon.

Boil it till the tomatas are all to pieces, and the ochras entirely dissolved. Strain it, and then serve it up with toasted bread cut into dice, put in after it comes out of the pot.

This soup will be improved by a pint of shelled Lima beans, boiled by themselves, and put into the tureen just before you send it to table.

BEAN SOUP.

Put two quarts of dried white beans into soak the night before you make the soup, which should be put on as early in the day as possible.

Take five pounds of the lean of fresh beef—the coarse pieces will do. Cut them up, and put them into your soup-pot with the bones belonging to them, (which should be broken to pieces,) and a pound of bacon cut very small. If you have the remains of a piece of beef that has been roasted the day before, and so much under-done that the juices remain in it, you may put it into the pot, and its bones along with it. Season the meat with pepper and salt, and pour on it six quarts of water. As soon as it boils take off the scum, and put in the beans (having first drained them) and a head of celery cut small, or a table-spoonful of pounded celery-seed. Boil it slowly till the meat is done to shreds, and the beans all dissolved. Then strain it through a cullender into the tureen, and put into it small squares of toasted bread with the crust cut off.

Some prefer it with the beans boiled soft, but not quite dissolved. In this case, do not strain it; but take out the meat and bones with a fork before you send it to table.

PEAS SOUP.

Soak two quarts of dried or split peas overnight. In the morning take three pounds of the lean of fresh beef, and a pound of bacon or pickled pork. Cut them into pieces, and put them into a large soup-pot with the peas, (which must first be well drained,) and a table-spoonful of dried mint rubbed to powder. Add five quarts of water, and boil the soup gently for three hours, skimming it well, and then put in four heads of celery cut small, or two table-spoonfuls of pounded celery seed.

It must be boiled till the peas are entirely dissolved, so as to be no longer distinguishable, and the celery quite soft. Then strain it into a tureen, and serve it up with toasted bread cut in dice. Omit the crust of the bread.

Stir it up immediately before it goes to table, as it is apt to settle, and be thick at the bottom and thin at the top.

GREEN PEAS SOUP.

Take four pounds of knuckle of veal, and a pound of bacon. Cut them to pieces, and put them into a soup kettle with a sprig of mint and four quarts of water. Boil it moderately fast, and skim it well. When the meat is boiled to rags, strain it out, and put to the liquor a quart of young green peas. Boil them till they are entirely dissolved, and till they have thickened the soup, and given it a green colour. [Footnote: You may greatly improve the colour by pounding a handful of spinach in a mortar, straining the juice, and adding it to the soup about a quarter of an hour before it has done boiling.]

Have ready two quarts of green peas that have been boiled in another pot with a sprig of mint, and two or three lumps of loaf sugar, (which will greatly improve the taste.) After they have boiled in this pot twenty minutes, take out the mint, put the whole peas into the pot of soup, and boil all together about ten minutes. Then put it into a tureen, and send it to table.

Never use hard old green peas for this soup, or for any other purpose. When they begin to turn yellow, it is time to leave them off for the season.

Lima bean soup may be made in the same manner.

ASPARAGUS SOUP.

Asparagus soup may be made in a similar manner to that of green peas. You must have four or five bunches of asparagus. Cut off the green tops, and put half of them into the soup, after the meat has been boiled to pieces and strained out. The asparagus must be boiled till quite dissolved, and till it has given a green colour to the soup. Then take the remainder of the asparagus tops (which must all this time have been lying in cold water) and put them into the soup, and let them boil about twenty minutes. Serve it up with small squares of toast in the tureen.

You may heighten the green of this soup by adding the juice of a handful of spinach, pounded in a mortar and strained. Or you may colour it with the juice of boiled spinach squeezed through a cloth. The spinach juice should be put in fifteen or ten minutes before you take up the soup, as a short boiling in it will take off the peculiar taste.

FRIAR'S CHICKEN.

Cut up four pounds of knuckle of veal; season it with white pepper and salt: put it into a soup-pan and let it boil slowly till the meat drops from the bone. Then strain it off. Have ready a pair of young fowls skinned, and cut up as you carve them at table. Season them with white pepper, salt, and mace. Put them into the soup, add a handful of chopped parsley, and let them boil. When the pieces of chicken are all quite tender, have ready four or five eggs well beaten. Stir the egg into the soup, and take it immediately off the fire lest it curdle. Serve up the chicken in the soup.

Rabbits may be substituted for fowls.

CATFISH SOUP.

Catfish that have been caught near the middle of the river are much nicer than those that are taken near the shore where they have access to impure food. The small white ones are the best. Having cut off their heads, skin the fish, and clean them, and cut them in three. To twelve small catfish allow a pound and a half of ham. Cut the ham into small pieces, or slice it very thin, and scald it two or three times in boiling water, lest it be too salt. Chop together a bunch of parsley and some sweet marjoram stripped from the stalks. Put these ingredients into a soup kettle and season them with pepper: the ham will make it salt enough. Add a head of celery cut small, or a large table-spoonful of celery seed tied up in a bit of clear muslin to prevent its dispersing. Pat in two quarts of water, cover the kettle, and let it boil slowly till every thing is sufficiently done, and the fish and ham quite tender. Skim it frequently. Boil in another vessel a quart of rich milk, in which you have melted a quarter of a pound of butter divided into small bits and rolled in flour. Pour it hot to the soup, and stir in at the last the beaten yolks of four eggs. Give it another boil, just to take off the rawness of the eggs, and then put it into a tureen, taking out the bag of celery seed before you send the soup to table, and adding some toasted bread cut into small squares. In making toast for soap, cut the bread thick, and pare off all the crust.

This soup will be found very fine.

Eel soup may be made in the same manner: chicken soup also.

LOBSTER SOUP.

Have ready a good broth made of a knuckle of veal boiled slowly in as much water as will cover it, till the meat is reduced to rags. It must then be well strained.

Having boiled three fine middle-sized lobsters, extract all the meat from the body and claws. Bruise part of the coral in a mortar, and also an equal quantity of the meat. Mix them well together. Add mace, nutmeg, cayenne, and a little grated lemon-peel; and make them up into force-meat balls, binding the mixture with the yolk of an egg slightly beaten.

Take three quarts of the veal broth, and put into it the meat of the lobsters cut into mouthfuls. Boil it together about twenty minutes. Then thicken it with the remaining coral, (which you must first rub through a sieve,) and add the force-meat balls, and a little butter rolled in flour. Simmer it gently for ten minutes, but do not let it come to a boil, as that will injure the colour. Pour it into a tureen, and send it to table immediately.

OYSTER SOUP.

To two quarts of oysters add a pint of water, and let them set an hour. Then take them out of the liquor. Grate and roll fine a dozen crackers. Put them into the liquor with a large lump of fresh butter. When the grated biscuit has quite dissolved, add a quart of milk with a grated nutmeg, and a dozen blades of mace; and, if in season, a head of celery split fine and cut into small pieces. Season it to your taste with pepper.

Mix the whole together, and set it in a closely covered vessel over a slow fire. When it comes to a boil, put in the oysters; and when it comes to a boil again, they will be sufficiently done.

Before you send it to table put into the tureen some toasted bread cut into small squares, omitting the crust.

PLAIN OYSTER SOUP.

Take two quarts of large oysters. Strain their liquor into a soup pan; season it with a tea-spoonful of whole pepper, a tea-spoonful of whole allspice, the same quantity of whole cloves, and seven or eight blades of mace. If the oysters are fresh, add a large tea-spoonful of salt; if they are salt oysters, none is requisite. Set the pan on hot coals, and boil it slowly (skimming it when necessary) till you find that it is sufficiently flavoured with the taste of the spice. In the mean time (having cut out the hard part) chop the oysters fine, and season them with a powdered nutmeg. Take the liquor from the fire, and strain out the spice from it. Then return it to the soup pan, and put the chopped oysters into it, with whatever liquid may have continued about them. Add a quarter of a pound of butter, divided into little bits and rolled in flour. Cover the pan, and let it boil hard about five minutes. If oysters are cooked too much they become tough and tasteless.

CLAM SOUP.

Having put your clams into a pot of boiling water to make them open easily, take them from the shells, carefully saving the liquor. To the liquor of a quart of opened clams, allow three quarts of water. Mix the water with the liquor of the clams and put it into a large pot with a knuckle of veal, the bone of which should be chopped in four places. When it has simmered slowly for four hours, put in a large bunch of sweet herbs, a beaten nutmeg, a tea-spoonful of mace, and a table-spoonful of whole pepper, but no salt, as the salt of the clam liquor will be sufficient. Stew it slowly an hour longer, and then strain it. When you have returned the liquor to the pot, add a quarter of a pound of butter divided into four and each bit rolled in flour. Then put in the clams, (having cut them, in pieces,) and let it boil fifteen minutes. Send it to table with toasted bread in it cut into dice.

This soup will be greatly improved by the addition of small force-meat balls. Make them of cold minced veal or chicken, mixed with equal quantities of chopped suet and sweet marjoram, and a smaller proportion of hard-boiled egg, grated lemon-peel, and powdered nutmeg. Pound all the ingredients together in a mortar, adding a little pepper and salt. Break in a raw egg or two (in proportion to the quantity) to bind the whole together and prevent it from crumbling to pieces. When thoroughly mixed, make the force-meat into small balls, and let them boil ten minutes in the soup, shortly before you send it to table. If you are obliged to make them of raw veal or raw chicken they must boil longer.

It will be a great improvement to cut up a yam and boil it in the soup.

Oyster soup may be made in this manner.

PLAIN CLAM SOUP.

Take a hundred clams, well washed, and put them into a large pot of boiling water. This will cause the shells to open. As they open take them out, and extract the clams, taking care to save the liquor. Mix with the liquor a quart of water, (or what will be much better, a quart of milk,) and thicken it with butter rolled in flour. Add a large bunch of parsley tied up, and a large table-spoonful of whole pepper. Put the liquid into a pot over a moderate fire. Make some little round dumplings (about the size of a hickory nut) of flour and butter, and put them into the soup. When it comes to a boil, put in the clams, and keep them boiling an hour. Take them out before you send the soup to table.

When the soup is done, take out the bunch of parsley. Have ready some toasted bread cut into small squares or dice. Put it into the soup before you send it to table.

You may make oyster soup in a similar manner.

WATER SOUCHY.

Cut up four flounders, or half a dozen perch, two onions, and a bunch of parsley. Put them into three quarts of water, and boil them till the fish go entirely to pieces, and dissolve in the water. Then strain the liquor through a sieve, and put it into a kettle or stew-pan. Have ready a few more fish with the heads, tails, and fins removed, and the brown skin taken off. Cut little notches in them, and lay them for a short time in very cold water. Then put them into the stew-pan with the liquor or soup-stock of the first fish. Season with pepper, salt, and mace, and add half a pint of white wine or two table-spoonfuls of vinegar. Boil it gently for a quarter of an hour, and skim it well.

Provide some parsley roots, cut into slices and boiled till very tender; and also a quantity of parsley leaves boiled nice and green. After the fish-pan has boiled moderately fifteen minutes, take it off the fire, and put in the parsley roots; also a little mushroom catchup.

Take out the fish and lay them in a broad deep dish, or in a tureen, and then pour on the soup very gently for fear of breaking them. Strew the green parsley leaves over the top. Have ready plates of bread and butter, which it is customary to eat with water souchy.

You may omit the wine or vinegar, and flavour the soup just before you take it from the fire with essence of anchovy, or with any other of the essences and compound fish-sauces that are in general use.

Water souchy (commonly pronounced *sookey*) is a Dutch soup. It may be made of any sort of small fish; but flounders and perch are generally used for it. It is very good made of carp.

FISH.

REMARKS.

In choosing fresh fish, select only those that are thick and firm, with bright scales and stiff fins; the gills a very lively red, and the eyes full and prominent. In the summer, as soon as they are brought home, clean them, and put them in ice till you are ready to cook them; and even then do not attempt to keep a fresh fish till next day. Mackerel cannot be cooked too soon, as they spoil more readily than any other fish.

Oysters in the shell may be kept from a week to a fortnight, by the following process. Cover them with water, and wash them clean with a birch broom. Then lay them with the deep or concave part of the shell undermost, and sprinkle each of them well with salt and Indian meal. Fill up the tub with cold water. Repeat this every day; first pouring off the liquid of the day before.

The tub must stand all the time in a cool cellar, and be covered well with an old blanket, carpeting, or something of the sort.

If carefully attended to, oysters kept in this manner will not only live but fatten.

It is customary to eat fish only at the commencement of the dinner. Fish and soup are generally served up alone, before any of the other dishes appear, and with no vegetable but potatoes; it being considered a solecism in good taste to accompany them with any of the other productions of the garden except a little horseradish, parsley, &c. as garnishing.

In England, and at the most fashionable tables in America, bread only is eaten with fish. To this rule salt cod is an exception.

TO BOIL FRESH SALMON

Scale and clean the fish, handling it as little as possible, and cutting it open no more than is absolutely necessary. Place it on the strainer of a large fish-kettle and fill it up with cold water. Throw in a handful of salt. Let it boil slowly. The length of time depends on the size and weight of the fish. You may allow a quarter of an hour to each pound; but experience alone can determine the exact time. It must however be thoroughly done, as nothing is more disgusting than fish that is under-cooked. You may try it with a fork. Skim it well or the colour will be bad.

The minute it is completely boiled, lift up the strainer and rest it across the top of the kettle, that the fish may drain, and then, if you cannot send it to table immediately, cover it with a soft napkin or flannel several folds double, to keep it firm by absorbing the moisture.

Send it to table on a hot dish. Garnish with scraped horseradish and curled parsley. Have ready a small tureen of lobster sauce to accompany the salmon.

Take what is left of it after dinner, and put it into a deep dish with a close cover. Having saved some of the water in which the fish was boiled, take a quart of it, and season it with half an ounce of whole pepper, and half an ounce of whole allspice, half a pint of the best vinegar, and a tea-spoonful of salt. Boil it; and when cold, pour it over the fish, and cover it closely again. In a cold place, and set on ice, it will keep a day or two, and may be eaten at breakfast or supper.

If much of the salmon has been left, you must proportion a larger quantity of the pickle.

Boil salmon trout in a similar manner.

TO BAKE FRESH SALMON WHOLE

Having cleaned a small or moderate sized salmon, season it with salt, pepper, and powdered mace rubbed on it both outside and in. Skewer it with the tail turned round and put to the mouth. Lay it on a stand or trivet in a deep dish or pan, and stick it over with bits of butter rolled in flour. Put it into the oven, and baste it occasionally, while baking, with its own drippings.

Garnish it with horseradish and sprigs of curled parsley, laid alternately round the edge of the dish; and send to table with it a small tureen of lobster sauce.

Salmon trout may be drest in the same manner.

SALMON BAKED IN SLICES.

Take out the bone and cut the flesh into slices. Season them with cayenne and salt. Melt two ounces of butter that has been rolled in flour, in a half pint of water, and mix with it two large glasses of port wine, two tablespoonfuls of catchup, and two anchovies. This allowance is for a small quantity of salmon. For a large dish you must proportion the ingredients accordingly. Let the anchovies remain in the liquid till they are dissolved. Then strain it and pour it over the slices of salmon. Tie a sheet of buttered paper over the dish, and put it into the oven.

You may bake trout or carp in the same manner.

SALMON STEAKS

Split the salmon and take out the bone as nicely as possible, without mangling the flesh. Then cut it into fillets or steaks about an inch thick. Dry them lightly in a cloth, and dredge them with flour. Take care not to squeeze or press them. Have ready some clear bright coals, such as are fit for beef-steaks. Let the gridiron be clean and bright, and rub the bars with chalk to prevent the fish from sticking. Broil the slices thoroughly, turning them with steak tongs. Send them to table hot, wrapped in the folds of a napkin that has been heated. Serve up with them anchovy, or prawn, or lobster sauce.

Many epicures consider this the best way of cooking salmon.

Another way, perhaps still nicer, is to take some pieces of white paper and butter them well. Wrap in each a slice of salmon, securing the paper around them, with a string or pins. Lay them on a gridiron, and broil them over a clear but moderate fire, till thoroughly done. Take off the paper, and send the cutlets to table hot, garnished with fried parsley.

Serve up with them prawn or lobster sauce in a boat.

PICKLED SALMON.

Take a fine fresh salmon, and having cleaned it, cut it into large pieces, and boil it in salted water as if for eating. Then drain it, wrap it in a dry cloth, and set it in a cold place till next day. Then make the pickle, which must be in proportion to the quantity of fish. To one quart of the water in which the salmon was boiled, allow two quarts of the best vinegar, one ounce of whole black pepper, one ounce of whole allspice, and a dozen blades of mace. Boil all these together in a kettle closely covered to prevent the flavour from evaporating. When the vinegar thus prepared is quite cold, pour it over the salmon, and put on the top a table-spoonful of sweet oil, which will make it keep the longer.

Cover it closely, put it in a dry cool place, and it will be good for many months.

This is the nicest way of preserving salmon, and is approved by all who have tried it. Garnish with fennel.

SMOKED SALMON.

Cut the fish up the back; clean, and scale it, and take out the roe, but do not wash it. Take the bone neatly out. Rub it well inside and out with a mixture of salt and fine Havanna sugar, in equal quantities, and a small portion of saltpetre. Cover the fish with a board on which weights are placed to press it down, and let it lie thus for two days and two nights. Drain it from the salt, wipe it dry, stretch it open, and fasten it so with pieces of stick. Then hang it up and smoke it over a wood fire. It will be smoked sufficiently in five or six days.

When you wish to eat it, cut off slices, soak them awhile in lukewarm water, and broil them for breakfast.

TO BOIL HALIBUT.

Halibut is seldom cooked whole; a piece weighing from four to six pounds being generally thought sufficient. Score deeply the skin of the back, and when you put it into the kettle lay it on the strainer with the back undermost. Cover it with cold water, and throw in a handful of salt. Do not let it come to a boil too fast. Skim it carefully, and when it has boiled hard a few minutes, hang the kettle higher, or diminish the fire under it, so as to let it simmer for about twenty-five or thirty minutes. Then drain it, and send it to table, garnished with alternate heaps of grated horseradish and curled parsley, and accompanied by a boat of egg-sauce.

What is left of the halibut, you may prepare for the supper-table by mincing it when cold, and seasoning it with a dressing of salt, cayenne, sweet oil, hard-boiled yolk of egg, and a large proportion of vinegar.

HALIBUT CUTLETS.

Cut your halibut into steaks or cutlets about an inch thick. Wipe them with a dry cloth, and season them with salt and cayenne pepper. Have ready a pan of yolk of egg well beaten, and a large flat dish of grated bread crumbs.

Put some fresh lard or clarified beef dripping into a frying pan, and hold it over a clear fire till it boils. Dip your cutlets into the beaten egg, and then into the bread crumbs. Fry them of a light brown. Serve them up hot, with the gravy in the bottom of the dish.

Salmon or any large fish may be fried in the same manner.

Halibut cutlets are very fine cut quite thin and fried in the best sweet oil, omitting the egg and bread crumbs.

TO BROIL MACKEREL.

Mackerel cannot be eaten in perfection except at the sea-side, where it can be had immediately out of the water. It loses its flavour in a very few hours, and spoils sooner than any other fish. Broiling is the best way of cooking it.

Clean two fine fresh mackerel, and wipe them dry with a cloth. Split them open and rub them with salt. Spread some very bright coals on the hearth, and set the gridiron over them well greased. Lay on the mackerel, and broil them very nicely, taking care not to let them burn. When one side is quite done, turn them on the other. Lay them, on a hot dish, and butter and pepper them before they go to table. Garnish them with lumps or pats of minced paisley mixed with butter, pepper and salt.

BOILED MACKEREL.

Clean the mackerel well, and let them lie a short time in vinegar and water. Then put them into the fish-kettle with cold water and a handful of salt. Boil them slowly. If small, they will be sufficiently cooked in twenty minutes. When the eye starts and the tail splits they are done. Take them up immediately on finding them boiled enough. If they stand any time in the water they will break.

Serve them up with parsley sauce, and garnish the dish with lumps of minced parsley.

They are eaten with mustard.

For boiling, choose those that have soft roes.

Another way is to put them in cold salt and water, and let them warm gradually for an hour. Then give them one hard boil, and they will be done.

TO BOIL SALT CODFISH.

The day previous to that on which it is to be eaten, take the fish about four o'clock in the afternoon, and put it into a kettle of cold water. Then place it within the kitchen fire-place, so as to keep it blood-warm. Next morning at ten, take out the fish, scrub it clean with a hard brash, and put it into a kettle of fresh cold water, into which a jill of molasses has been stirred. The molasses will be found an improvement. Place the kettle again near the fire, until about twenty minutes before dinner. Then hang it over the fire, and boil it hard a quarter of an hour, or a little more.

When done, drain it, and cut it into large pieces. Wrap them closely in a fine napkin and send them to table on a large dish, garnished round the edge with hard-boiled eggs, either cut in half, or in circular slices, yolks and whites together. Have ready in a small tureen, egg-sauce made with, drawn butter, thickened with hard-boiled eggs chopped fine. Place on one side of the fish a dish of mashed potatoes, on the other a dish of boiled parsnips.

The most usual way of preparing salt cod for eating when it comes to table, is (after picking out all the bones) to mince it fine on your plate, and mix it with mashed potato, parsnip, and egg-sauce; seasoning it to your taste with cayenne and mustard. What is left may be prepared for breakfast nest morning. It should be put into a skillet or spider, which must be well buttered inside, and set over hot coals to warm and brown. Or it may be made up into small cakes and fried.

You may add to the mixture onions boiled and chopped.

TO BOIL FRESH COD.

Having washed and cleaned the fish, leave out the roe and liver; rub some salt on the inside, and if the weather is very cold you may keep it till next day. Put sufficient water in the fish-kettle to cover the fish very well, and add to the water a large handful of salt. As soon as the salt is entirely melted put in the fish. A very small codfish will be done in about twenty minutes, (after the water has boiled;) a large one will take half an hour, or more. Garnish with the roe and liver fried, or with scraped horseradish. Send it to table with oyster-sauce in a boat. Or you may make a sauce by flavouring your melted butter with a glass of port wine, and an anchovy boned and minced.

ANOTHER WAY OF BOILING FRESH COD.

Put the fish into cold water with a handful of salt, and let it slowly and gradually warm for three hours if the cod is large, and two hours if it is small. Then increase the fire, and boil it hard for a few minutes only.

BAKED SHAD.

Keep on the head and fins. Make a force-meat or stuffing of grated bread crumbs, cold boiled ham or bacon minced fine, sweet marjoram, pepper, salt, and a little powdered mace or cloves. Moisten it with beaten yolk of egg. Stuff the inside of the fish with it, reserving a little to rub over the outside, having first rubbed the fish all over with yolk of egg. Lay the fish in a deep pan, putting its tail to its mouth. Pour into the bottom of the pan a little water, and add a jill of port wine, and a piece of butter rolled in flour. Bake it well, and when it is done, send it to table with the gravy poured round it. Garnish with slices of lemon.

Any fish may be baked in the same manner.

A large fish of ten or twelve pounds weight, will require about two hours baking.

TO BROIL A SHAD.

Split and wash the shad, and afterwards dry it in a cloth. Season it with salt and pepper. Have ready a bed of clear bright coals. Grease your gridiron well, and as soon as it is hot lay the shad upon it, and broil it for about a. quarter of an hour or more, according to the thickness. Butter it well, and send it to table. You may serve with it melted butter in a sauce-boat.

Or you may cut it into three pieces and broil it without splitting. It will then, of course, require a longer time. If done in this manner, send it to table with melted butter poured over it.

BOILED ROCK-FISH.

Having cleaned the rock-fish, put it into a fish-kettle with water enough to cover it well, having first dissolved a handful of salt in the water. Set it over a moderate fire, and do not let it boil too fast. Skim it well.

When done, drain it, and put it on a large dish. Have ready a few eggs boiled hard. Cut them in half, and lay them closely on the back of the fish in a straight line from the head to the tail. Send with it in a boat, celery sauce flavoured with a little cayenne.

SEA BASS OR BLACK FISH.

May be boiled and served up in the above manner.

PICKLED ROCK-FISH.

Have ready a large rock-fish. Put on your fish-kettle with a sufficiency of water to cover the fish amply; spring or pump water is best. As soon as the water boils, throw in a tea-cup full of salt, and put in the fish. Boil it gently for about half an hour, skimming it well. Then take it out, and drain it, laying it slantingly. Reserve a part of the water in which the fish has been boiled, and season it to your taste with whole cloves, allspice, and mace. Boil it up to extract the strength from the spice, and after it has boiled add to it an equal quantity of the best vinegar. You must have enough of this liquid to cover the fish again. When the fish is quite cold, cut off the head and tail, and cut the body into large pieces, extracting the back-bone. Put it into a stone jar, and when the spiced liquor is cold, pour it on the fish, cover the jar closely, and set it in a cool place. It will be fit for use in a day or two, and if well secured from the air, and put into a cold place will keep a fortnight.

FRIED PERCH.

Having cleaned the fish and dried them, with a cloth, lay them, side by side, on a board or large dish; sprinkle them with salt, and dredge them with flour. After a while turn them, and salt and dredge the other side. Put some lard or fresh beef-dripping into a frying-pan, and hold it over the fire. When the lard boils, put in the fish and fry them of a yellowish brown. Send to table with them in a boat, melted butter flavoured with anchovy.

Flounders or other small fish may be fried in the same manner.

You may know when the lard or dripping is hot enough, by dipping in the tail of one of the fish. If it becomes crisp immediately, the lard is in a proper state for frying. Or you may try it with a piece of stale bread which will become brown directly, if the lard is in order.

There should always be enough of lard to cover the fish entirely. After they have fried five minutes on one side, turn them and fry them five minutes on the other. Skim the lard or dripping always before you put in the fish.

TO FRY TROUT.

Having cleaned the fish, and cut off the fins, dredge them with flour. Have ready some beaten yolk of egg, and in a separate dish some grated bread crumbs. Dip each fish into the egg, and then strew them with bread crumbs. Put some butter or fresh beef-dripping into a frying-pan, and hold it over the fire till it is boiling hot; then, (having skimmed it,) put in the fish and fry them.

Prepare some melted butter with a spoonful of mushroom-catchup and a spoonful of lemon-pickle stirred into it. Send it to table in a sauce-boat to eat with the fish.

You may fry carp and flounders in the same manner.

TO BOIL TROUT.

Put a handful of salt into the water. When it boils put in the trout. Boil them fast about twenty minutes, according to their size.

For sauce, send with them melted butter, and put some soy into it; or flavour it with catchup.

FRIED SEA BASS.

Score the fish on the back with a knife, and season them with salt and cayenne pepper. Cut some small onions in round slices, and chop fine a bunch of parsley. Put some butter into a frying-pan over the fire, and when it is boiling hot lay in the fish. When they are about half done put the onions and parsley into the pan. Keep turning the fish that the onions and parsley may adhere to both sides. When quite done, put them into the dish in which they are to go to table, and garnish the edge of the dish with hard boiled eggs cut in round slices.

Make in the pan in which they have been fried, a gravy, by adding some butter rolled in flour, and a small quantity of vinegar. Pour it into the dish with the fish.

STURGEON CUTLETS OR STEAKS.

This is the most approved way of dressing sturgeon. Carefully take off the skin, as its oiliness will give the fish a strong and disagreeable taste when cooked. Cut from the tail-piece slices about half an inch thick, rub them with salt, and broil them over a clear fire of bright coals. Butter them, sprinkle them with cayenne pepper, and send them to table hot, garnished with sliced lemon, as lemon-juice is generally squeezed over them when eaten.

Another way is to make a seasoning of bread-crumbs, sweet herbs, pepper and salt. First dip the slices of sturgeon, in beaten yolk of egg, then cover them with seasoning, wrap them up closely in sheets of white paper well buttered, broil them over a clear fire, and send them to table either with or without the papers.

STEWED CARP.

Having cut off the head, tail, and fins, season the carp with salt, peppers and powdered mace, both, inside and out. Rub the seasoning on very well, and let them lay in it an hour, Then put them into a stew-pan with a little parsley shred fine, a whole onion, a little sweet marjoram, a tea-cup of thick cream or very rich milk, and a lump of butter rolled in flour. Pour in sufficient water to cover the carp, and let it stew half an hour.

Perch may be done in the same way.

You may dress a piece of sturgeon in this manner, but you must first boil it for twenty minutes to extract the oil. Take off the skin before you proceed to stew the fish.

CHOWDER.

Take a pound or more of salt pork, and having half boiled it, cut it into slips, and with some of them cover the bottom of a pot. Then strew on some sliced onion. Have ready a large fresh cod, or an equal quantity of haddock, tutaug, or any other firm fish. Cut the fish into large pieces, and lay part of it on the pork and onions. Season it with pepper. Then cover it with a layer of biscuit, or crackers that have been previously soaked in milk or water. You may add also a layer of sliced potatoes.

Next proceed with a second layer of pork, onions, fish, &c. and continue as before till the pot is nearly full; finishing with soaked crackers. Pour in about a pint and a half of cold water. Cover it close, set it on hot coals, and let it simmer about an hour. Then skim it, and turn it out into a deep dish. Leave the gravy in the pot till you have thickened it with a piece of butter rolled in flour, and some chopped parsley. Then give it one boil up, and pour it hot into the dish.

Chowder may be made of clams, first cutting off the hard part.

SHELL FISH

PICKLED OYSTERS.

Take a hundred and fifty fine large oysters, and pick off carefully the bits of shell that may be sticking to them. Lay the oysters in a deep dish, and then strain the liquor over them. Put them into an iron skillet that is lined with porcelain, and add salt to your taste. Without salt they will not be firm enough. Set the skillet on hot coals, and allow the oysters to simmer till they are heated all through, but not till they boil. Then take out the oysters and put them into a stone jar, leaving the liquor in the skillet. Add to it a pint of clear strong vinegar, a large tea-spoonful of blades of mace, three dozen whole cloves, and three dozen whole pepper corns. Let it come to a boil, and when the oysters are quite cold in the jar, pour the liquor oh them.

They are fit for use immediately, but are better the next day. In cold weather they will keep a week.

If you intend sending them a considerable distance you must allow the oysters to boil, and double the proportions of the pickle and spice.

FRIED OYSTERS.

Get the largest and finest oysters. After they are taken from the shell wipe each of them quite dry with a cloth. Then beat up in a pan yolk of egg and milk, (in the proportion of two yolks to half a jill or a wine glass of milk,) and grate some stale broad grated very fine in a large flat dish. Cut up at least half a pound of fresh butter in the frying-pan, and hold it over the fire till it is boiling hot. Dip the oysters all over lightly in the mixture of egg and milk, and then roll them up and down in the grated bread, making as many crumbs stick to them as you can.

Put them into the frying-pan of hot butter, and keep it over a hot fire. Fry them brown, turning them that they may be equally browned on both sides. If properly done they will be crisp, and not greasy.

Serve them, dry in a hot dish, and do not pour over them the butter that may be left in the pan when they are fried.

Oysters are very good taken out of the shells and broiled on a gridiron.

SCOLLOPED OYSTERS.

Having grated a sufficiency of stale bread, butter a deep dish, and line the sides and bottom thickly with bread crumbs. Then put in a layer of seasoned oysters, with a few very small bits of butter on them. Cover them thickly with crumbs, and put in another layer of oysters and butter, till the dish is filled up, having a thick layer of crumbs on the top. Put the dish into an oven, and bake them a very short time, or they will shrivel. Serve them up hot.

You may bake them in large clam shells, or in the tin scollop shells made for the purpose. Butter the bottom of each shell; sprinkle it with bread crumbs; lay on the oysters seasoned with cayenne and nutmeg, and put a morsel of butter on each. Fill up the shells with a little of the oyster liquor thickened with bread crumbs, and set them on a gridiron over coals, browning them afterwards with a red-hot shovel.

STEWED OYSTERS.

Put the oysters into a sieve, and set it on a pan to drain the liquor from them. Then cut off the hard part, and put the oysters into a stew-pan with some whole pepper, a few blades of mace, and some grated nutmeg. Add a small piece of butter rolled in flour. Then pour over them about half of the liquor, or a little more. Set the pan on hot coals, and simmer them gently about five minutes. Try one, and if it tastes raw cook them a little longer. Make some thin slices of toast, having cut off all the crust. Butter the toast and lay it in the bottom of a deep dish. Put the oysters upon it with the liquor in which they were stewed.

The liquor of oysters should never be thickened by stirring in flour. It spoils the taste, and gives them a sodden and disagreeable appearance, and is no longer practised by good cooks.

OYSTER FRITTERS.

Have ready some of the finest and largest oysters; drain them from the liquor and wipe them dry.

Beat six eggs very light, and stir into them gradually six table-spoonfuls of line sifted flour. Add by degrees a pint and a half of rich milk and some grated nutmeg, and beat it to a smooth batter.

Make your frying-pan very hot, and put into it a piece of butter or lard. When it has melted and begins to froth, put in a small ladle-full of the batter, drop an oyster in the middle of it, and fry it of a light brown. Send them to table hot.

If you find your batter too thin, so that it spreads too much in the frying-pan, add a little more flour beaten well into it. If it is too thick, thin it with some additional milk.

OYSTER PIE.

Make a puff-paste, in the proportion of a pound and a half of fresh butter to two pounds of sifted flour. Roll it out rather thick, into two sheets. Butter a deep dish, and line the bottom and sides of it with paste. Fill it up with crusts of bread for the purpose of supporting the lid while it is baking, as the oysters will be too much done if they are cooked in the pie. Cover it with the other sheet of paste, having first buttered the flat rim of the dish. Notch the edges of the pie handsomely, or ornament them with leaves of paste which you may form with tin cutters made for the purpose. Make a little slit in the middle of the lid, and stick firmly into it a paste tulip or other flower. Put the dish into a moderate oven, and while the paste is baking prepare the oysters, which should he large and fresh. Put them into a stew-pan with half their liquor thickened with yolk of egg boiled hard and grated, enriched with pieces of butter rolled in bread crumbs, and seasoned with mace and nutmeg. Stew the oysters five minutes. When the paste is baked, carefully take off the lid, remove the pieces of bread, and put in the oysters and gravy. Replace the lid, and send the pie to table warm.

TO BOIL A LOBSTER.

Put a handful of salt into a large kettle or pot of boiling water. When the water boils very hard put in the lobster, having first brushed it, and tied the claws together with a bit of twine. Keep it boiling from half an hour to an hour in proportion to its size. If boiled too long the meat will be hard and stringy. When it is done, take it out, lay it on its claws to drain, and then wipe it dry. Send it to table cold, with the body and tail split open, and the claws taken off. Lay the large claws next to the body, and the small ones outside. Garnish with double parsley.

It is scarcely necessary to mention that the head of a lobster, and what are called the lady-fingers are not to be eaten.

TO DRESS LOBSTER COLD.

Put a table-spoonful of cold water on a clean plate and with the back of a wooden spoon mash into it the coral or scarlet meat of the lobster, adding a salt-spoonful of salt, and about the same quantity of cayenne. On another part of the plate mix well together with the back of the spoon two table-spoonfuls of sweet oil, and a tea-spoonful of made mustard. Then mix the whole till they are well incorporated and perfectly smooth, adding, at the last, three table-spoonfuls of vinegar.

This quantity of seasoning is for a small lobster. For a large one, more of course will be required. Many persons add a tea-spoonful of powdered white sugar, thinking that it gives a mellowness to the whole.

The meat of the body and claws of the lobster must be carefully extracted from the shell and minced very small When the dressing is smoothly and thoroughly amalgamated mix the meat with it, and let it be handed round to the company.

The vinegar from a jar of Indian pickle is by some preferred for lobster dressing.

You may dress the lobster immediately *before* you send it to table. When the dressing and meat are mixed together, pile it in a deep dish, and smooth it with the back of a spoon. Stick a bunch of the small claws in the top, and garnish with curled parsley.

Very large lobsters are not the best, the meat being coarse and tough.

STEWED LOBSTER.

Having boiled the lobster, extract the meat from the shell, and cut it into very small pieces. Season it with a powdered nutmeg, a few blades of mace, and cayenne and salt to your taste. Mix with it a quarter of a pound of fresh butter cut small, and two glasses of white wine or of vinegar. Put it into a stew-pan, and set it on hot coals. Stew it about twenty minutes, keeping the pan closely covered lest the flavour should evaporate. Serve it up hot.

If you choose, you can send it to table in the shell, which must first be nicely cleaned. Strew the meat over with sifted bread-crumbs, and brown the top with a salamander, or a red hot shovel held over it.

FRICASSEED LOBSTER.

Put the lobster into boiling salt and water, and let it boil according to its size from a quarter of an hour to half an hour. The intention is to have it parboiled only, as it is afterwards to be fricasseed. Extract the meat from the shell, and cut it into small pieces. Season it with white pepper, salt, and nutmeg; and put it into a stew-pan with as much cream as will cover it. Keep the lid close; set the pan on hot coals, and stew it slowly for about as long a time as it was previously boiled. Just before you take it from the fire, stir in the beaten yolk of an egg. Send it to table in a small dish placed on a larger one, and arrange the small claws nicely round it on the large dish.

POTTED LOBSTER.

Parboil the lobster in boiling water well salted. Then pick out all the meat from the body and claws, and beat it in a mortar with nutmeg, mace, cayenne, and salt, to your taste. Beat the coral separately. Then put the pounded meat into a large potting can of block tin with a cover. Press it down hard, having arranged it in alternate layers of white meat and coral to give it a marbled or variegated appearance. Cover it with fresh butter, and put it into a slow oven for half an hour. When cold, take off the butter and clarify it, by putting it into a jar, which, must be set in a pan of boiling water. Watch it well, and when it melts, carefully skim off the buttermilk which will rise to the top. When no more scum rises, take it off and let it stand for a few minutes to settle, and then strain it through a sieve.

Put the lobster into small potting-cans, pressing it down very hard. Pour the clarified butter over it, and secure the covers tightly.

Potted lobster is used to lay between thin slices of bread as sandwiches. The clarified butter that accompanies it is excellent for fish sauce.

Prawns and crabs may be potted in a similar manner.

LOBSTER PIE.

Put two middle-sized lobsters into boiling salt and water. When they are half boiled, take the meat from the shell, cut it into very small pieces, and put it into a pie dish. Break up the shells, and stew them in a very little water with half a dozen blades of mace and a wine-glass of vinegar. Then strain off the liquid. Beat the coral in a mortar, and thicken the liquid with it. Pour this into the dish of lobster to make the gravy. Season it with cayenne, salt, and mushroom catchup, and add bits of butter. Cover it with a lid of paste, made in the proportion of half a pound of butter to a pound of flour, notched handsomely, and ornamented with paste leaves. Do not send it to table till it has cooled.

TO BOIL PRAWNS.

Throw a handful of salt into a pot of boiling water. When it boils very hard, put in the prawns. Let them boil a quarter of an hour, and when you take them out lay them on a sieve to drain, and then wipe them on a dry cloth, and put them aside till quite cold.

Lay a handful of curled parsley in the middle of a dish. Put one prawn on the top of it, and lay the others, all round, as close as you can, with the tails outside. Garnish with parsley.

Eat them with salt, cayenne, sweet oil, mustard and vinegar, mixed together as for lobsters.

CRABS

Crabs are boiled in the same manner, and in serving up may be arranged like prawns.

HOT CRABS.

Having boiled the crabs, extract all the meat from the shell, cut it fine, and season it to your taste with nutmeg, salt, and cayenne pepper. Add a bit of butter, some grated bread crumbs, and sufficient vinegar to moisten it.

Fill the back-shells of the crab with the mixture; set it before the fire, and brown it by holding a red-hot shovel or a salamander a little above it.

Cover a large dish, with small slices of dry toast with the crust cut off. Lay on each slice a shell filled with the crab. The shell of one crab will contain the meat of two.

COLD CRABS.

Having taken all the meat out of the shells, make a dressing with sweet oil, salt, cayenne pepper, mustard and vinegar, as for lobster. You may add to it some hard-boiled yolk of egg, mashed in the oil. Put the mixture into the back shells of the crabs, and serve it up. Garnish with the small claws laid nicely round.

SOFT CRABS.

These crabs must be cooked directly, as they will not keep till next day.

Remove the spongy substance from each side of the crab, and also the little sand-bag. Put some lard into a pan, and when it is boiling hot, fry the crabs in it. After you take them out, throw in a handful of parsley, and let it crisp; but withdraw it before it loses its colour. Strew it over the crabs when you dish them.

Make the gravy by adding cream or rich milk to the lard, with some chopped parsley, pepper and salt. Let them all boil together for a few minutes, and then serve it up in a sauce-boat.

TERRAPINS.

Have ready a pot of boiling water. When it is boiling very hard put in the terrapins, and let them remain in it till quite dead. Then take them out, pull off the outer skin and the toe-nails, wash the terrapins in warm water and boil them again, allowing a tea-spoonful of salt to each terrapin. When the flesh becomes quite tender so that you can pinch it off, take them out of the shell, remove the sand-bag, and the gall, which you must be careful not to break, as it will make the terrapin so bitter as to be uneatable. Cut up all the other parts of the inside with the meat, and season it to your taste with black and cayenne pepper, and salt. Put all into a stew-pan with the juice or liquor that it has given out in cutting up, but not any water. To every two terrapins allow a quarter of a pound of butter divided into pieces and rolled in flour, two glasses of Madeira, and the yolks of two eggs. The eggs must be beaten, and not stirred in till a moment before it goes to table. Keep it closely covered. Stew it gently till every thing is tender, and serve it up hot in a deep dish.

Terrapins, after being boiled by the cook, may be brought to table plain, with all the condiments separate, that the company may dress them according to taste.

For this purpose heaters or chafing-dishes must be provided for each plate.

PICKLED LOBSTER.

Take half a dozen fine lobsters. Put them into boiling salt and water, and when they are all done, take them out and extract all the meat from the shells, leaving that of the claws as whole as possible, and cutting the flesh of the body into large pieces nearly of the same size. Season a sufficient quantity of vinegar very highly with whole pepper-corns, whole cloves, and whole blades of mace. Put the pieces of lobster into a stew-pan, and pour on just sufficient vinegar to keep them well covered. Set it over a moderate fire; and when it has boiled hard about five minutes, take out the lobster, and let the pickle boil by itself for a quarter of an hour. When the pickle and lobster are both cold, put them together into a broad flat stone jar. Cover it closely, and set it away in a cool place.

Eat the pickled lobster with oil, mustard, and vinegar, and have bread and butter with it.

BEEF.

GENERAL REMARKS.

When beef is good, it will have a fine smooth open grain, and it will feel tender when squeezed or pinched in your fingers. The lean should be of a bright carnation red, and the fat white rather than yellow—the suet should be perfectly white. If the lean looks dark or purplish, and the fat very yellow, do not buy the meat.

See that the butcher has properly jointed the meat before it goes home. For good tables, the pieces generally roasted are the sirloin and the fore and middle ribs. In genteel houses other parts are seldom served up as *roast-beef*. In small families the ribs are the most convenient pieces. A whole sirloin is too large, except for a numerous company, but it is the piece most esteemed.

The best beef-steaks are those cut from the ribs, or from the inner part of the sirloin. All other pieces are, for this purpose, comparatively hard and tough.

The round is generally corned or salted, and boiled. It is also used for the dish called beef à-la-mode.

The legs make excellent soup; the head and tail are also used for that purpose.

The tongue when fresh is never cooked except for mince-pies. Corned or salted it is seldom liked, as in that state it has a faint sickly taste that few persons can relish. But when pickled and afterwards smoked (the only good way of preparing a tongue) it is highly and deservedly esteemed.

The other pieces of the animal are generally salted and boiled. Or when fresh they may be used for soup or stews, if not too fat.

If the state of the weather will allow you to keep fresh beef two or three days, rub it with salt, and wrap it in a cloth.

In summer do not attempt to keep it more than twenty-four hours; and not then unless you can conveniently lay it in ice, or in a spring-house.

In winter if the beef is brought from market frozen, do not cook it that day unless you dine very late, as it will be impossible to get it sufficiently done—meat that has been frozen requiring double the usual time. To thaw it, lay it in cold water, which is the only way to extract the frost without injuring the meat. It should remain in the water three hours, or more.

TO ROAST BEEF.

The fire should be prepared at least half an hour before the beef is put down, and it should be large, steady, clear, and bright, with plenty of fine hot coals at the bottom.

The best apparatus for the purpose is the well-known roaster frequently called a tin-kitchen.

Wash the meat in cold water, and then wipe it dry, and rub it with salt. Take care not to run the spit through the best parts of it. It is customary with some cooks to tie blank paper over the fat, to prevent it from melting and wasting too fast.

Put it evenly into the roaster, and do not set it too near the fire, lest the outside of the meat should be burned before the inside is heated.

Put some nice beef-dripping or some lard into the pan or bottom of the roaster, and as soon as it melts begin to baste the beef with it; taking up the liquid with a long spoon, and pouring it over the meat so as to let it trickle down again, into the pan. Repeat this frequently while it is roasting; after a while you can baste it with its own fat. Turn the spit often, so that the meat may be equally done on all sides.

Once or twice draw back the roaster, and improve the fire by clearing away the ashes, bringing forward the hot coals, and putting on fresh fuel at the back. Should a coal fall into the dripping-pan take it out immediately. An allowance of about twenty minutes to each pound of meat is the time commonly given for roasting; but this rule, like most others, admits of exceptions according to circumstances. Also, some persons like their meat very much done; others prefer it rare, as it is called. In summer, meat will roast in a shorter time than in winter.

When the beef is nearly done, and the steam draws towards the fire, remove the paper that has covered the fat part, sprinkle on a little salt, and having basted the meat well with the dripping, pour off nicely (through the spout of the roaster) all the liquid fat from the top of the gravy.

Lastly, dredge the meat very lightly with a little flour, and baste it with fresh butter. This will give it a delicate froth. To the gravy that is now running from the meat add nothing but a tea-cup of boiling water. Skim it, and send it to table in a boat. Serve up with the beef in a small deep plate, scraped horseradish moistened with vinegar.

Fat meat requires more roasting than lean, and meat that has been frozen will take nearly double the usual time.

Basting the meat continually with flour and water is a bad practice, as it gives it a coddled parboiled appearance, and diminishes the flavour.

These directions for roasting beef will apply equally to mutton.

Pickles are generally eaten with roast beef. French mustard is an excellent condiment for it. In carving begin by cutting a slice from the side.

TO SAVE BEEF-DRIPPING.

Pour off through the spout of the roaster or tin-kitchen, all the fat from the top of the gravy, after you have done basting the meat with it. Hold a little sieve under the spout, and strain the dripping through it into a pan. Set it away in a cool place; and next day when it is cold and congealed, turn the cake of fat, and scrape with a knife the sediment from the bottom. Pat the dripping into a jar; cover it tightly, and set it away in the refrigerator, or in the coldest place you have. It will be found useful for frying, and for many other purposes.

Mutton-dripping cannot be used for any sort of cooking, as it communicates to every thing the taste of tallow.

BAKED BEEF.

This is a plain family dish, and is never provided for company.

Take a nice but not a fat piece of fresh beef. Wash it, rub it with salt, and place it on a trivet in a deep block tin or iron pan. Pour a little water into the bottom, and put under and round the trivet a sufficiency of pared potatoes, either white or sweet ones. Put it into a hot oven, and let it bake till thoroughly done, basting it frequently with its own gravy. Then transfer it to a hot dish, and serve up the potatoes in another. Skim the gravy, and send it to table in a boat.

Or you may boil the potatoes, mash them with milk, and put them into the bottom of the pan about half an hour before the meat is done baking. Press down the mashed potatoes hard with the back of a spoon, score them in cross lines over the top, and let them, brown under the meat, serving them up laid round it.

Instead of potatoes, you may put in the bottom of the pan what is called a Yorkshire pudding, to be baked under the meat.

To make this pudding,—stir gradually four table-spoonfuls of flour into a pint of milk, adding a salt-spoon of salt. Beat three eggs very light, and mix them gradually with the milk and flour. See that the batter is not lumpy. Do not put the pudding under the meat at first, as if baked too long it will be hard and solid. After the meat has baked till the pan is quite hot and well greased with the drippings, you may put in the batter; having continued stirring it till the last moment.

If the pudding is so spread over the pan as to be but an inch thick, it will require about two hours baking, and need not be turned. If it is thicker than an inch, you must (after it is brown on the top) loosen it in the pan, by inserting a knife beneath it, and having cut it across into four pieces, turn them all nicely that the other side may be equally done. But this pudding is lighter and better if laid so thin as not to require turning.

When you serve up the beef lay the pieces of pudding round it, to be eaten with the meat.

Veal may be baked in this manner with potatoes or a pudding. Also fresh pork.

TO BOIL CORNED OR SALTED BEEF.

The best piece is the round. You may either boil it whole, or divide it into two, or even three pieces if it is large, taking care that each piece shall have a portion of the fat. Wash it well; and, if very salt, soak it in two waters. Skewer it up tightly and in a good compact shape, wrapping the flap piece firmly round it. Tie it round with broad strong tape, or with a strip of coarse linen. Put it into a large pot, and cover it well with water. It will be found a convenience to lay it on a fish drainer.

Hang it over a moderate fire that it may heat gradually all through. Carefully take off the scum as it rises, and when no more appears, keep the pot closely covered, and let it boil slowly and regularly, with the fire at an equal temperature. Allow three hours and a half to a piece weighing about twelve pounds, and from that to four or five hours in proportion to the size. Turn the meat twice in the pot while it is boiling. Put in some carrots and turnips about two hours after the meat. Many persons boil cabbage in the same pot with the beef, but it is a much nicer way to do the greens in a separate vessel, lest they become saturated with the liquid fat. Cauliflower or brocoli (which are frequent accompaniments to corned beef) should never be boiled with it.

Wash the cabbage in cold water, removing the outside leaves, and cutting the stalk close. Examine all the leaves carefully, lest insects should be lodged among them. If the cabbage is large, divide it into quarters. Put it into a pot of boiling water with a handful of salt, and boil it till the stalk is quite tender. Half an hour will generally be sufficient for a small young cabbage; an hour for a large full-grown one. Drain it well before you dish it. If boiled separately from the meat, have ready some melted butter to eat with it.

Should you find the beef under-done, you may reboil it next day; putting it into boiling-water and letting it simmer for half an hour or more, according to its size.

Cold corned beef will keep very well for some days wrapped in several folds of a thick linen cloth, and set away in a cool dry place.

In carving a round of beef, slice it horizontally and very thin. Do not help any one to the outside pieces, as they are generally too hard and salt. French mustard is very nice with corned beef. [Footnote: French mustard is made of the very best mustard powder, diluted with vinegar, and flavoured with minced tarragon leaves, and a minced clove of garlic; all mixed with a wooden spoon.]

This receipt will apply equally to any piece of corned beef, except that being less solid than the round, they will, in proportion to their weight, require rather less time to boil.

In dishing the meat, remove the wooden skewers and substitute plated or silver ones.

Many persons think it best (and they are most probably right) to stew corned beef rather than to boil it. If you intend to stew it, put no more water in the pot than will barely cover the meat, and keep it gently simmering over a slow fire for four, five, or six hours, according to the size of the piece.

TO BROIL BEEF-STEAKS.

The best beef-steaks are those cut from the ribs or from the inside of the sirloin. All other parts are for this purpose comparatively hard and tough.

They should be cut about three quarters of an inch thick, and, unless the beef is remarkably fine and tender, the steaks will be much improved by beating them on both sides with a steak mallet, or with a rolling-pin. Do not season them till you take them from the fire.

Have ready on your hearth a fine bed of clear bright coals, entirely free from smoke and ashes. Set the gridiron over the coals in a slanting direction, that the meat may not be smoked by the fat dropping into the fire directly under it. When the gridiron is quite hot, rub the bars with suet, sprinkle a little salt over the coals, and lay on the steaks. Turn them frequently with a pair of steak-tongs, or with a knife and fork. A quarter of an hour is generally sufficient time to broil & beef-steak. For those who like them under-done or rare, ten or twelve minutes will be enough.

When the fat blazes and smokes very much as it drips into the fire, quickly remove the gridiron for a moment, till the blaze has subsided. After they are browned, cover the upper side of the steaks with an inverted plate or dish to prevent the flavour from evaporating. Rub a dish with a shalot or small onion, and place it near the gridiron and close to the fire, that it may be well heated. In turning the steak drop the gravy that may be standing on it into this dish, to save it from being lost. When the steaks are done, sprinkle them with a little salt and pepper, and lay them in a hot dish, putting on each a piece of fresh butter. Then, if it is liked, season them with, a very little raw shalot, minced as finely as possible, and moistened with a spoonful of water; and stir a tea-spoonful of catchup into the gravy. Send the steaks to table very hot, in a covered dish. You may serve up with them onion sauce in a small tureen.

Pickles are frequently eaten with beef-steaks.

Mutton chops may be broiled in the same manner.

TO FRY BEEF-STEAKS.

Beef-steaks for frying should be cut thinner than for broiling. Take them from the ribs or sirloin, and remove the bone. Beat them to make them tender. Season them with salt and pepper.

Put some fresh butter, or nice beef-dripping into a frying pan, and hold it over a clear bright fire till it boils and has done hissing. Then put in the steaks, and (if you like them) some sliced onions. Fry them about a quarter of an hour, turning them frequently. Steaks, when fried, should be thoroughly done. After they are browned, cover them with a large plate to keep in the juices,

Have ready a hot dish, and when they are done, take out the steaks and onions and lay them in it with another dish on the top, to keep them hot while you give the gravy in the pan another boil up over the fire. You may add to it a spoonful of mushroom catchup. Pour the gravy over the steakes, and send them to table as hot as possible.

Mutton chops may be fried in this manner.

BEEF-STEAK PUDDING.

For a small pudding take a pound of fresh beef suet. Clear it from the skin and the stringy fibres, and mince it as finely as possible. Sift into a large pan two pounds of fine flour, and add the suet gradually, rubbing it fine with your hands and mixing it thoroughly. Then pour in, by degrees, enough of cold water to make a stiff dough. Roll it out into a large even sheet. Have ready about a pound and a half of the best beef-steak, omitting the bone and fat which should be all cut off. Divide the steak into small thin pieces, and beat them well to make them tender. Season them with pepper and salt, and, if convenient, add some mushrooms. Lay the beef in the middle of the sheet of paste, and put on the top a bit of butter rolled in flour. Close the paste nicely over the meat as if you were making a large dumpling. Dredge with flour a thick square cloth, and tie the pudding up in it, leaving space for it to swell. Fasten the string very firmly, and stop up with flour the little gap at the tying-place so that no water can get in. Have ready a large pot of boiling water. Put the pudding into it, and let it boil fast three hours or more. Keep up a good fire under it, as if it stops boiling a minute the crust will be heavy. Have a kettle of boiling water at the fire to replenish the pot if it wastes too much. Do not take up the pudding till the moment before it goes to table. Mix some catchup with the gravy on your plate.

For a large pudding you must have two pounds of suet, three pounds of flour, and two pounds and a half of meat. It must boil at least five hours.

All the fat must be removed from the meat before it goes into the pudding, as the gravy cannot be skimmed when enclosed in the crust.

You may boil in the pudding some potatoes cut into slices.

A pudding of the lean of mutton chops may be made in the same manner; also of venison steaks.

A BEEF-STEAK PIE.

Make a good paste in the proportion of a pound of butter to two pounds of sifted flour. Divide it in half, and line with one sheet of it the bottom and sides of a deep dish, which must first be well buttered. Have ready two pounds of the best beef-steak, cut thin, and well beaten; the bone and fat being omitted. Season it with pepper and salt. Spread a layer of the steak at the bottom of the pie, and on it a layer of sliced potato, and a few small bits of butter rolled in flour. Then another layer of meat, potato, &c., till the dish is full. You may greatly improve the flavour by adding mushrooms, or chopped clams or oysters, leaving out the hard parts. If you use clams or oysters, moisten the other ingredients with a little of their liquor. If not, pour in, at the last, half a pint of cold water, or less if the pie is small. Cover the pie with the other sheet of paste as a lid, and notch the edges handsomely, having reserved a little of the paste to make a flower or tulip to stick in the slit at the top. Bake it in a quick oven an hour and a quarter, or longer, in proportion to its size. Send it to table hot.

You may make a similar pie of mutton chops, or veal cutlets, or venison steaks, always leaving out the bone and fat.

Many persons in making pies stew the meat slowly in a little water till about half done, and they then put it with its gravy into the paste and finish by baking. In this case add no water to the pie, as there will be already sufficient liquid If you half-stew the meat, do the potatoes with it.

A-LA-MODE BEEF.

Take the bone out of a round of fresh beef, and beat the meat well all over to make it tender. Chop and mix together equal quantities of sweet marjoram and sweet basil, the leaves picked from the stalks and rubbed fine. Chop also some small onions or shalots, and some parsley; the marrow from the bone of the beef; and a quarter of a pound, or more of suet. Add two penny rolls of stale bread grated; and pepper, salt, and nutmeg to your taste. Mix all these ingredients well, and bind them together with the beaten yolks of four eggs. Fill with this seasoning the place from whence you took out the bone; and rub what is left of it all over the outside of the meat. You must, of course, proportion the quantity of stuffing to the size of the round of beef. Fasten it well with skewers, and tie it round firmly with a piece of tape, so as to keep it compact and in good shape. It is best to prepare the meat the day before it is to be cooked.

Cover the bottom of a stew-pan with slices of bacon. Lay the beef upon them, and cover the top of the meat with more slices of bacon. Place round it four large onions, four carrots, and four turnips, all cut in thick slices. Pour in from half a pint to a pint of water, and if convenient, add two calves' feet cut in half. Cover the pan closely, set it in an oven and let it bake for at least six hours; or seven or eight, according to the size.

When it is thoroughly done, take out the beef and lay it on a dish with the vegetables round it. Remove the bacon and calves' feet, and (having skimmed the fat from the gravy carefully) strain it into a small sauce-pan; set it on hot coals, and stir into it a tea-cupful of port wine, and the same quantity of pickled mushrooms. Let it just come to a boil, and then send it to table in a sauce-tureen.

If the beef is to be eaten cold, you may ornament it as follows:— Glaze it all over with beaten white of egg. Then cover it with a coat of boiled potato grated finely. Have ready some slices of cold boiled carrot, and also of beet-root. Cut them into the form of stars or flowers, and arrange them handsomely over the top of the meat by sticking them on the grated potato. In the centre place a large bunch of double parsley, interspersed with flowers cut out of raw turnips, beets, and carrots, somewhat in imitation of white and red roses, and marygolds. Fix the flowers on wooden skewers concealed with parsley.

Cold à-la-mode beef prepared in this manner will at a little distance look like a large iced cake decorated with sugar flowers.

You may dress a fillet of veal according to this receipt. Of course it will require less time to stew.

TO STEW BEEF.

Take a good piece of fresh beef. It must not be too fat. Wash it, rub it with salt, and put it into a pot with barely sufficient water to cover it. Set it over a slow fire, and after it has stewed an hour, put in some potatoes pared and cut in half, and some parsnips, scraped and split. Let them stew with the beef till quite tender. Turn the meat several times in the pot. When all is done, serve up the meat and vegetables together, and the gravy in a boat, having first skimmed it.

This is a good family dish.

You may add turnips (pared and sliced) to the other vegetables.

Fresh pork may be stewed in this manner, or with sweet potatoes.

TO STEW A ROUND OF BEEF.

Trim off some pieces from a round of fresh beef—take out the bone and break it. Put the bone and the trimmings into a pan with some cold water, and add an onion, a carrot, and a turnip all cut in pieces, and a bunch, of sweet herbs. Simmer them for an hour, and having skimmed it well, strain off the liquid. Season the meat highly with what is called kitchen pepper, that is, a mixture, in equal quantities, of black or white pepper, allspice, cinnamon, cloves, ginger and nutmeg, all finely powdered. Fasten it with skewers, and tie it firmly round with tape. Lay skewers in the bottom of the stew-pan; place the beef upon them, and then pour over it the gravy you have prepared from the bone and trimmings. Simmer it about an hour and a half, and then turn the meat over, and add to it three carrots, three turnips, and two onions all sliced, and a glass of tarragon vinegar. Keep the lid close, except when you are skimming off the fat. Let the meat stew till it is thoroughly done and tender throughout. The time will depend on the size of the round. It may require from five or six to eight hours.

Just before you take it up, stir into the gravy a table-spoonful or two of mushroom catchup, a little made mustard, and a piece of butter rolled in flour.

Send it to table hot, with the gravy poured round it.

ANOTHER WAY TO STEW A ROUND OF BEEF,

Take a round of fresh beef (or the half of one if it is very large) and remove the bone. The day before you cook it, lay it in a pickle made of equal proportions of water and vinegar with salt to your taste. Next morning take it out of the pickle, put it into a large pot or stew-pan, and just cover it with water. Put in with it two or three large onion a few cloves, a little whole black pepper, and a large glass of port or claret. If it is a whole round of beef allow two glasses of wine. Stew it slowly for at least four hours or more, in proportion to its size. It must be thoroughly done, and tender all through. An hour before you send it to table take the meat out of the pot, and pour the gravy into a pan. Put a large lump of butter into the pot, dredge the beef with flour, and return it to the pot to brown, turning it often to prevent its burning. Or it will be better to put it into a Dutch oven. Cover the lid with hot coals, renewing them as they go out. Take the gravy that you poured from the meat, and skim off all the fat. Put it into a sauce-pan, and mix with it a little butter rolled in flour, and add some more cloves and wine. Give it a boil up. If it is not well browned, burn some sugar on a hot shovel, and stir it in.

If you like it stuffed, have ready when you take the meat out of the pickle, a force-meat of grated bread crumbs, sweet herbs, butter, spice, pepper and salt, and minced parsley, mixed with beaten yolk of egg. Fill with this the opening from whence you took the bone, and bind a tape firmly round the meat.

BEEF BOUILLI.

Take part of a round of fresh beef (or if you prefer it a piece of the flank or brisket) and rub it with salt. Place skewers in the bottom of the stew-pot, and lay the meat upon them with barely water enough to cover it. To enrich the gravy you may add the necks and other trimmings of whatever poultry you may happen to have; also the root of a tongue, if convenient. Cover the pot, and set it over a quick fire. When it boils and the scum has risen, skim it well, and then diminish the fire so that the meat shall only simmer; or you may set the pot on hot coals. Then put in four or five carrots sliced thin, a head of celery cut up, and four or fire sliced turnips. Add a bunch of sweet herbs, and a small table-spoonful of black pepper-corns tied in a thin muslin rag. Let it stew slowly for four or fire hours, and then add a dozen very small onions roasted and peeled, and a large table-spoonful of capers or nasturtians. You may, if you choose, stick a clove in each onion. Simmer it half an hour longer, then take up the meat, and place-it in a dish, laying the vegetables round it. Skim and strain the gravy; season it with catchup, and made mustard, and serve it up in a boat. Mutton may be cooked in this manner.

HASHED BEEF.

Take some roast beef that has been very much under-done, and having cut off the fat and skin, put the trimmings with the bones broken up into a stew-pan with two large onions sliced, a few sliced potatoes, and a bunch of sweet herbs. Add about a pint of warm water, or broth if you have it. This is to make the gravy. Cover it closely, and let it simmer for about an hour. Then skim and strain it, carefully removing every particle of fat.

Take another stew-pot, and melt in it a piece of butter, about the size of a large walnut. When it has melted, shake in a spoonful of flour. Stir it a few minutes, and then add to it the strained gravy. Let it come to a boil, and then put to it a table-spoonful of catchup, and the beef cut either in thin small slices or in mouthfuls. Let it simmer from five to ten minutes, but do not allow it to boil, lest (having been cooked already) it should become tasteless and insipid. Serve it up in a deep dish with thin slices of toast cut into triangular or pointed pieces, the crust omitted. Dip the toast in the gravy, and lay the pieces in regular order round the sides of the dish.

You may hash mutton or veal in the same manner, adding sliced carrots, turnips, potatoes, or any vegetables you please. Tomatas are an improvement.

To hash cold meat is an economical way of using it; but there is little or no nutriment in it after being twice cooked, and the natural flavour is much impaired by the process.

Hashed meat would always be much better if the slices were cut from the joint or large piece as soon as it leaves the table, and soaked in the gravy till next day.

BEEF CAKES.

Take some cold roast beef that has been under-done, and mince it very fine. Mix with it grated bread crumbs, and a little chopped onion and parsley. Season it with pepper and salt, and moisten it with some beef-dripping and a little walnut or onion pickle. Some scraped cold tongue or ham will be found an improvement. Make it into broad flat cakes, and spread a coat of mashed potato thinly on the top and bottom of each. Lay a small bit of butter on the top of every cake, and set them in an oven to warm and brown.

Beef cakes are frequently a breakfast dish.

Any other cold fresh meat may be prepared in the same manner.

Cold roast beef may be cut into slices, seasoned with salt and pepper, broiled a few minutes over a clear fire, and served up hot with a little butter spread on them.

TO ROAST A BEEF'S HEART.

Cut open the heart, and (having removed the ventricles) soak it in cold water to free it from the blood, Parboil it about ten minutes. Prepare, a force-meat of grated bread crumbs, butter or minced suet, sweet marjoram and parsley chopped fine, a little grated lemon-peel, nutmeg, pepper, and salt to your taste, and some yolk of egg to bind the ingredients. Stuff the heart with the force-meat, and secure the opening by tying a string around it. Put it on a spit, and roast it till it is tender throughout.

Add to the gravy a piece of butter rolled in flour, and a glass of red wine. Serve up the heart very hot in a covered dish. It chills immediately.

Eat currant jelly with it.

Boiled beef's heart is frequently used in mince pies.

TO STEW A BEEF'S HEART.

Clean the heart, and cut it lengthways into large pieces. Put them into a pot with a little salt and pepper, and cover them with cold water. Parboil them for a quarter of an hour, carefully skimming off the blood that rises to the top. Then take them out, cut them, into mouthfuls, and having strained the liquid, return them to it, adding a head or two of chopped celery, a few sliced onions, a dozen potatoes pared and quartered, and a piece of butter rolled in flour. Season with whole pepper, and a few cloves if you like. Let it stew slowly till all the pieces of heart and the vegetables are quite tender.

You may stew a beef's kidney in the same manner.

The heart and liver of a calf make a good dish cooked as above.

TO DRESS BEEF KIDNEY.

Having soaked a fresh kidney in cold water and dried it in a cloth, cut it into mouthfuls, and then mince it fine. Dust it with flour. Put some butter into a stew-pan over a moderate fire, and when it boils put in the minced kidney. When you have browned it in the butter, sprinkle on a little salt and cayenne pepper, and pour in a very little boiling water. Add a glass of champagne or other wine, or a large tea-spoonful of mushroom catchup, or of walnut pickle. Cover the pan closely, and let it stew till the kidney is tender. Send it to table hot in a covered dish. It is eaten generally at breakfast.

TO BOIL TRIPE.

Wash it well in warm water, and trim it nicely, taking off all the fat. Cut it into small pieces, and put it on to boil five hours before dinner, in water enough to cover it very well. After it has boiled four hours, pour off the water, season the tripe with pepper and salt, and put it into a pot with milk and water mixed in equal quantities. Boil it an hour in the milk and water.

Boil in a sauce-pan ten or a dozen onions. When they are quite soft, drain them in a cullender, and mash them. Wipe out your sauce-pan and put them on again, with a bit of butter rolled in flour, and a wine-glass of cream or milk. Let them boil up, and add them to the tripe just before you send it to table. Eat it with pepper, vinegar, and mustard.

TRIPE AND OYSTERS.

Having boiled the tripe in milk and water, for four or five hours till it is quite tender, gut it up into small pieces. Put it into a stew-pan with just milk enough to cover it, and a few blades of mace. Let it stew about five minutes, and then put in the oysters, adding a large piece of butter rolled-in flour, and salt and cayenne pepper to your taste. Let it stew five minutes longer, and then send it to table in a tureen; first skimming off whatever fat may float on the surface.

TO FRY TRIPE.

Boil the tripe the day before, till it is quite tender, which it will not be in less than four or five hours. Then cover it and set it away. Next day cut it into long slips, and dip each piece into beaten yolk of egg, and afterwards roll them in grated bread crumbs. Have ready in a frying-pan over the fire, some good beef-dripping. When it is boiling hot put in the tripe, and fry it about ten minutes, till of a light brown.

You may serve it up with onion sauce.

Boiled tripe that has been left from the dinner of the preceding day may be fried in this manner.

PEPPER POT.

Take four pounds of tripe, and four ox feet. Put them into a large pot with as much water as will cover them, some whole pepper, and a little salt. Hang them over the fire early in the morning. Let them boil slowly, keeping the pot closely covered. When the tripe is quite tender, and the ox feet boiled to pieces, take them out, and skim the liquid and strain it. Then cut the tripe into small pieces; put it back into the pot, and pour the soup or liquor over it. Have ready some sweet herbs chopped fine, some sliced onions, and some sliced potatoes. Make some small dumplings with flour and batter. Season the vegetables well with pepper and salt, and put them into the pot. Have ready a kettle of boiling water, and pour on as much as will keep the ingredients covered while boiling, but take care not to weaken the taste by putting too much water. Add a large piece of butter rolled in flour, and lastly put in the dumplings. Let it boil till all the things are thoroughly done, and then serve it up in the tureen.

TO BOIL A SMOKED TONGUE.

In buying dried tongues, choose those that are thick and plump, and that have the smoothest skins. They are the most likely to be young and tender.

A smoked tongue should soak in cold water at least all night. One that is very hard and dry will require twenty-four hours' soaking. When you boil it put it into a pot full of cold water. Set it over a slow fire that it may heat gradually for an hour before it comes to a boil. Then keep it simmering from three and a half to four hours, according to its size and age. Probe it with a fork, and do not take it up till it is tender throughout. Send it to table with mashed potato laid round it, and garnish with parsley. Do not split it in half when you dish it, as is the practice with some cooks. Cutting it lengthways spoils the flavour, and renders it comparatively insipid.

If you wish to serve up the tongue very handsomely, rub it with yolk of egg after you take it from the pot, and strew over it grated bread crumbs; baste it with butter, and set it before the fire till it becomes of a light brown. Cover the root (which is always an unsightly object) with thick sprigs of double parsley; and (instead of mashed potato) lay slices of currant jelly all round the tongue.

TO BOIL A SALTED OR PICKLED TONGUE.

Put it into boiling water, and let it boil three hours or more, according to its size. When you take it out peel and trim it, and send it to table surrounded with mashed potato, and garnished with sliced carrot.

TO CORN BEEF.

Wash the beef well, after it has lain awhile in cold water. Then drain and examine it, take out all the kernels, and rub it plentifully with salt. It will imbibe the salt more readily after being washed. In cold weather warm the salt by placing it before the fire. This will cause it to penetrate the meat more thoroughly.

In summer do not attempt to corn any beef that has not been fresh killed, and even then it will not keep more than a day and a half or two days. Wash and dry it, and rub a great deal of salt well into it. Cover it carefully, and keep it in a cold dry cellar.

Pork is corned in the same manner.

TO PICKLE BEEF OR TONGUES.

The beef must be fresh killed, and of the best kind. You must wipe every piece well, to dry it from the blood and moisture. To fifty pounds of meat allow two pounds and a quarter of coarse salt, two pounds and a quarter of fine salt, one ounce and a half of saltpetre, one pound and a half of brown sugar, and one quart of molasses. Mix all these ingredients well together, boil and skim it for about twenty minutes, and when no more scum rises, take it from the fire. Have ready the beef in a large tub, or in a barrel; pour the brine gradually upon it with a ladle, and as it cools rub it well into every part of the meat. A molasses hogshead sawed in two is a good receptacle for pickled meat. Cover it well with a thick cloth, and look at it frequently, skimming off whatever may float on the top, and basting the meat with the brine. In about a fortnight the beef will be fit for use.

Tongues may be put into the same cask with the beef, one or two at a time, as you procure them from the butcher. None of them will be ready for smoking in less than six weeks; but they had best remain in pickle two or three months. They should not be sent to the smoke-house later than March. If you do them at home, they will require three weeks' smoking over a wood fire. Hang them with the root or large end upwards. When done, sew up each tongue tightly in coarse linen, and hang them up in a dark dry cellar.

Pickled tongues without smoking are seldom liked.

The last of October is a good time for putting meat into pickle. If the weather is too warm or too cold, it will not take the salt well.

In the course of the winter the pickle may probably require a second boiling with additional ingredients.

Half an ounce of pearl-ash added to the other articles will make the meat more tender, but many persons thinks it injures the taste.

The meat must always be kept completely immersed in the brine. To effect this a heavy board should be laid upon it.

DRIED OR SMOKED BEEF.

The best part for this purpose is the round, which you must desire the butcher to cut into four pieces. Wash the meat and dry it well in a cloth.

Grind or beat to powder an equal quantity of cloves and allspice, and having mixed them together, rub them well into the beef with your hand. The spice will be found a great improvement both to the taste and smell of the meat. Have ready a pickle made precisely as that in the preceding article. Boil and skim it, and (the meat having been thoroughly rubbed all over with the spice) pour on the pickle, as before directed. Keep the beef in the pickle at least six weeks, and then smoke it about three weeks.

Smoked beef is brought on the tea-table either shaved into thin chips without cooking, or chipped and fried with a little butter in a skillet, and served up hot.

This receipt for dried or smoked beef will answer equally well for venison ham, which is also used as a relish at the tea-table.

Mutton hams may be prepared in the same way.

POTTED BEEF.

Take a good piece of a round of beef, and cut off all the fat. Rub the lean well with salt, and let it lie two days. Then put it into a jar, and add to it a little water in the proportion of half a pint to three pounds of meat. Cover the jar as closely as possible, (the best cover will be a coarse paste or dough) and set it in a slow oven, or in a vessel of boiling water for about four hours. Then drain off all the gravy and set the meat before the fire that all the moisture may be drawn out. Pull or cut it to pieces and pound it for a long time in a mortar with pepper, allspice, cloves, mace, nutmeg, and oiled fresh butter, adding these ingredients gradually, and moistening it with a little of the gravy. You must pound it to a fine paste, or till it becomes of the consistence of cream, cheese.

Put it into potting cans, and cover it an inch thick with fresh butter that has been melted, skimmed, and strained. Tie a leather over each pot, and keep them closely covered. Set them in a dry place.

Game and poultry may be potted in this manner

VEAL.

GENERAL REMARKS.

The fore-quarter of a calf comprises the neck, breast, and shoulder: the hind-quarter consists of the loin, fillet, and knuckle. Separate dishes are made of the head, heart, liver, and sweet-bread. The flesh of good veal is firm and dry, and the joints stiff. The lean is of a very light delicate red, and the fat quite white. In buying the head see that the eyes look full, plump, and lively; if they are dull and sunk the calf has been killed too long. In buying calves' feet for jelly or soup, endeavour to get those that have been singed only and not skinned; as a great deal of gelatinous substance is contained in the skin. Veal should always be thoroughly cooked, and never brought to table rare or under-done, like beef or mutton. The least redness in the meat or gravy is disgusting.

Veal suet may be used as a substitute for that of beef; also veal-dripping.

TO ROAST A LOIN OF VEAL.

The loin is the best part of the calf. It is always roasted. See that your fire is clear and hot, and broad enough to brown both ends. Cover the fat of the kidney and the back with paper to prevent it from scorching. A large loin of veal will require *at least* four hours and a half to roast it sufficiently. At first set the roaster at a tolerable distance from the fire that the meat may heat gradually in the beginning; afterwards place it nearer. Put a little salt and water into the dripping-pan and baste the meat with it till the gravy begins to drop. Then baste with the gravy. When the meat is nearly done, move it close to the fire, dredge it with a very little flour, and baste it with butter. Skim the fat from the gravy, which should be thickened by shaking in a very small quantify of flour. Put it into a small sauce-pan, and set it on hot coals. Let it just come to a boil, and then send it to table in a boat. If the gravy is not in sufficient quantity, add to it about half a jill or a large wine-glass of boiling water.

In carving a loin of veal help every one to a piece of the kidney as far as it will go.

TO ROAST A BREAST OF VEAL.

A breast of veal will require about three hours and a half to roast. In preparing it for the spit, cover it with the caul, and skewer the sweet-bread to the back. Take off the caul when the meat is nearly done. The breast, being comparatively tough and coarse, is less esteemed than the loin and the fillet.

TO ROAST A FILLET OF VEAL.

Take out the bone, and secure with skewers the fat flap to the outside of the meat. Prepare a stuffing of fresh butter or suet minced fine, and an equal quantity of grated bread-crumbs, a large table-spoonful of grated lemon-peel, a table-spoonful of sweet marjoram chopped or rubbed to powder, a nutmeg grated, and a little pepper and salt, with a sprig of chopped parsley. Mix all these ingredients with beaten yolk of egg, and stuff the place from whence the bone was taken. Make deep cuts or incisions all over the top of the veal, and fill them with some of the stuffing. You may stick into each hole an inch of fat ham or salt pork, cut very thin.

Having papered the fat, spit the veal and put it into the roaster, keeping it at first not too near the fire. Put a little salt and water into the dripping-pan, and for awhile baste the meat with it. Then baste it with its own gravy. A fillet of veal will require four hours roasting. As it proceeds, place it nearer to the fire. Half an hour before it is done, remove the paper, and baste the meat with butter, having first dredged it very lightly with flour. Having skimmed the gravy, mix some thin melted butter with it.

If convenient, you may in making the stuffing, use a large proportion of chopped mushrooms that have been preserved in sweet oil, or of chopped pickled oysters. Cold ham shred fine will improve it.

You may stuff a fillet of veal entirely with sausage meat.

To accompany a fillet of veal, the usual dish is boiled ham or bacon.

A shoulder of veal may be stuffed and roasted in a similar manner.

TO STEW A BREAST OF VEAL.

Divide the breast into pieces according to the position of the bones. Put them into a stew-pan with a few slices of ham, some whole pepper, a bunch of parsley, and a large onion quartered. Add sufficient water to keep it from burning, and let it stew slowly till the meat is quite tender. Then put to it a quart or more of green peas that have boiled twenty minutes in another pot, and a piece of butter rolled in flour. Let all stew together a quarter of an hour longer. Serve it up, with the veal in the middle, the peas round it, and the ham laid on the peas.

You may stew a breast of veal with tomatas.

TO STEW A FILLET OF VEAL.

Take a fillet of veal, rub it with salt, and then with a sharp knife make deep incisions all over the surface, the bottom as well as the top and sides. Make a stuffing of grated stale bread, butter, chopped sweet marjoram, grated lemon-peel, nutmeg, pepper and salt, mixed up with beaten yolk of egg to bind and give it consistency. Fill the holes or incisions with the stuffing, pressing it down well with your fingers. Reserve some of the stuffing to rub all over the outside of the meat. Have ready some very thin slices of cold boiled ham, the fatter the better. Cover the veal with them, fastening them on with skewers. Put it into a pot, and stew it slowly in a very little water, just enough to cover it. It will take at least five hours to stew; or more, in proportion to its size. When done, take off the ham, and lay it round the veal in a dish.

You may stew with it a quart or three pints of young green peas, put in about an hour before dinner; add to them a little butter and pepper while they are stewing. Serve them up in the dish with the veal, laying the slices of ham upon them.

If you omit the ham, stew the veal entirely in lard.

TO STEW A KNUCKLE OF VEAL.

Lay four wooden skewers across the bottom of your stew-pan, and place the meat upon them; having first carefully washed it, and rubbed it with salt. Add a table-spoonful of whole pepper, the leaves from a bunch of sweet marjoram, a bunch of parsley leaves chopped, two onions peeled and sliced, and a piece of butter rolled in flour. Pour in two quarts of water. Cover it closely, and after it has come to a boil, lessen the fire, and let the meat only simmer for two hours or more. Before you serve it up, pour the liquid over it.

This dish will be greatly improved by stewing with it a few slices of ham, or the remains of a cold ham.

Veal when simply boiled is too insipid. To stew it is much better.

VEAL CUTLETS.

The best cutlets are those taken from the leg or fillet. Cut them about half an inch thick, and as large as the palm of your hand. Season them with pepper and salt. Grate some stale bread, and rub it through a cullender, adding to it chopped sweet marjoram, grated lemon-peel, and some powdered mace or nutmeg. Spread the mixture on a large flat dish. Have ready in a pan some beaten egg. First dip each cutlet into the egg, and then into the seasoning on the dish, seeing that a sufficient quantity adheres to both sides of the meat. Melt in your frying-pan, over a quick fire, some beef-dripping, lard, or fresh butter, and when it boils lay your cutlets in it, and fry them thoroughly; turning them on both sides, and taking care that they do not burn. Place them in a covered dish near the fire, while you finish the gravy in the pan, by first skimming it, and then shaking in a little flour and stirring it round. Pour the gravy hot round the cutlets, and garnish with little bunches of curled parsley.

You may mix with the bread crumbs a little saffron.

VEAL STEAKS.

Cut a neck of veal into thin steaks, and beat them to make them tender. For seasoning, mix together some finely chopped onion sprinkled with pepper and salt, and a little chopped parsley. Add some butter, and put it with the parsley and onion into a small sauce-pan, and set it on hot coals to stew till brown. In the mean, time, put the steaks on a hot gridiron (the bars of which have been rubbed with suet) and broil them well, over a bed of bright clear coals. When sufficiently done on one side turn them on the other. After the last turning, cover each steak with some of the seasoning from the sauce-pan, and let all broil together till thoroughly done.

Instead of the onions and parsley, you may season the veal steaks with chopped mushrooms, or with chopped oysters, browned in butter.

Have ready a gravy made of the scraps and trimmings of the veal, seasoned with pepper and salt, and boiled in a little hot water in the same sauce-pan in which the parsley and onions have been previously stewed. Strain the gravy when it has boiled long enough, and flavour it with catchup.

MINCED VEAL.

Take some cold veal, cut it into slices, and mince it very finely with a chopping-knife. Season it to your taste with pepper, salt, sweet marjoram rubbed fine, grated lemon-peel and nutmeg. Put the bones and trimmings into a sauce-pan with a little water, and simmer them over hot coals to extract the gravy from them. Then put the minced veal into a stew-pan, strain the gravy over it, add a piece of butter rolled in flour, and a little milk or cream. Let it all simmer together till thoroughly warmed, but do not allow it to boil lest the meat having been once cooked already, should become tasteless. When you serve it up, have ready some three-cornered pieces of bread toasted and buttered; place them all round the inside of the dish.

Or you may cover the mince with a thick layer of grated bread, moistened with a little butter, and browned on the top with a salamander, or a red hot shovel.

VEAL PATTIES.

Mince very fine a pound of the lean of cold roast veal, and half a pound of cold boiled ham, (fat and lean equally mixed.) Put it into a stew-pan with three ounces of butter divided into bits and rolled in flour, a jill of cream, and a jill of veal gravy. Season it to your taste with cayenne pepper and nutmeg, grated lemon-peel, and lemon-juice. Set the pan on hot coals, and let the ingredients simmer till well warmed, stirring them well to prevent their burning.

Have ready baked some small shells of puff-paste. Fill them with the mixture, and eat the patties either warm or cold.

VEAL PIE.

Take two pounds of veal cut from the loin, fillet, or the best end of the neck. Remove the bone, fat, and skin, and put them into a sauce-pan with half a pint of water to stew for the gravy. Make a good paste, allowing a pound of butter to two pounds of flour. Divide it into two pieces, roll it out rather thick and cover with one piece the sides and bottom of a deep dish. Put in a layer of veal, seasoned with pepper and salt, then a layer of cold ham sliced thin, then more veal, more ham, and so on till the dish is full; interspersing the meat with yolks of eggs boiled hard. If you can procure some small button mushrooms they will be found an improvement. Pour in, at the last, the gravy you have drawn from the trimmings, and put on the lid of the pie, notching the edge handsomely, and ornamenting the centre with a flower made of paste. Bake the pie at least two hours and a half.

You may make a very plain veal pie simply of veal chops, sliced onions, and potatoes pared and quartered. Season with pepper and salt, and fill up the dish with water.

CALF'S HEAD DREST PLAIN

Wash the head in warm water. Then lay it in clean hot water and let it soak awhile. This will blanch it. Take out the brains and the black part of the eyes. Tie the head in a cloth, and put it into a large fish-kettle, with plenty of cold water, and add some salt to throw up the scum, which must be taken off as it rises. Let the head boil gently about three hours.

Put eight or ten sage leaves, and as much parsley, into a small sauce-pan with a little water, and boil them half an hour. Then chop them fine, and set them ready on a plate. Wash the brains well in two warm waters, and then soak them for an hour in a basin of cold water with a little salt in it. Remove the skin and strings, and then put the brains into a stew-pan with plenty of cold water, and let them boil gently for a quarter of an hour, skimming them well. Take them out, chop them, and mix them with the sage and parsley leaves, two table-spoonfuls of melted butter, and the yolks of four hard-boiled eggs, and pepper and salt to your taste. Then put the mixture into a sauce-pan and set it on coals to warm.

Take up the head when it is sufficiently boiled, score it in diamonds, brush it all over with beaten egg, and strew it with a mixture of grated bread-crumbs, and chopped sage and parsley. Stick a few bits of butter over it, and set it in a Dutch oven to brown. Serve it up with the brains laid round it. Or you may send to table the brains and the tongue in a small separate dish, having first trimmed the tongue and cut off the roots. Have also parsley-sauce in a boat. You may garnish with very thin small slices of broiled ham, curled up.

If you get a calf's head with the hair on, sprinkle it all over with pounded rosin, and dip it into boiling water. This will make the hairs scrape off easily.

CALF'S HEAD HASHED.

Take a calf's head and a set of feet, and boil them until tender, having first removed the brains. Then cut the flesh off the head and feet in slices from the bone, and put both meat and bones into a stew-pan with a bunch of sweet herbs, some sliced onions, and pepper and salt to your taste; also a large piece of butter rolled in flour, and a little water. After it has stewed awhile slowly till the flavour is well extracted from the herbs and onions, take out the meat, season it a little with cayenne pepper, and lay it in a dish. Strain the gravy in which it was stewed, and stir into it two glasses of madeira, and the juice and grated peel of a lemon. Having poured some of the gravy over the meat, lay a piece of butter on the top, set it in an oven and bake it brown.

In the mean time, having cleaned and washed the brains (skinning them and removing the strings) parboil them in a sauce-pan, and then make them into balls with chopped sweet herbs, grated bread-crumbs, grated lemon-peel, nutmeg, and beaten yolk of egg. Fry them in lard and butter mixed; and send them to table laid round the meat (which should have the tongue placed on the top) and garnish with sliced lemon. Warm the remaining gravy in a small sauce-pan on hot coals, and stir into it the beaten yolk of an egg a minute before you take it from the fire. Send it to table in a boat.

CHITTERLINGS OR CALF'S TRIPE.

See that the chitterlings are very nice and white. Wash them, cut them into pieces, and put them into a stew-pan with pepper and salt to your taste, and about two quarts of water. Boil them two hours or more. In the mean time, peel eight or ten white onions, and throw them whole into a sauce-pan with plenty of water. Boil them slowly till quite soft; then drain them in a cullender, and mash them. Wipe out your sauce-pan, and put in the mashed onions with a piece of butter, two table-spoonfuls of cream or rich milk, some nutmeg, and a very little salt. Sprinkle in a little flour, set the pan on hot coals (keeping it well covered) and give it one boil up.

When the chitterlings are quite tender all through, take them up and drain them. Place in the bottom of a dish a slice or two of buttered toast with all the crust cut off. Lay the chitterlings on the toast, and send them to table with the stewed onions in a sauce-boat. When you take the chitterlings on your plate season them with pepper and vinegar.

This, if properly prepared, is a very nice dish.

TO FRY CALF'S FEET.

Having first boiled them till tender, cut them in two, and (having taken out the large bones) season the feet with pepper and salt, and dredge them well with flour. Strew some chopped parsley or sweet marjoram over them, and fry them of a light brown in lard or butter. Serve them up with parsley-sauce.

TO FRY CALF'S LIVER.

Cut the liver into thin slices. Season it with pepper, salt, chopped sweet herbs, and parsley. Dredge it with flour, and fry it brown in lard or dripping. See that it is thoroughly done before you send it to table. Serve it up with its own gravy.

Some slices of cold boiled ham fried with it will be found an improvement.

You may dress a calf's heart in the same manner.

LARDED CALF'S LIVER.

Take a calf's liver and wash it well. Cut into long slips the fat of some bacon or salt pork, and insert it all through the surface of the liver by means of a larding-pin. Put the liver into a pot with a table-spoonful of lard, a little water, and a few tomatas, or some tomata catchup; adding one large or two small onions minced fine, and some sweet marjoram leaves rubbed very fine. The sweet marjoram will crumble more easily if you first dry it before the fire on a plate.

Having put in all these ingredients, set the pot on hot coals in the corner of the fire-place, and keep it stewing, regularly and slowly, for four hours. Send the liver to table with the gravy round it.

TO ROAST SWEET-BREADS.

Take four fine sweet-breads, and having trimmed them nicely, parboil them, and then lay them in a pan of cold water till they become cool. Afterwards dry them in a cloth. Put some butter into a sauce-pan, set it on hot coals, and melt and skim it. When it is quite clear, take it off. Have ready some beaten egg in one dish, and some grated bread-crumbs in another. Skewer each sweet-bread, and fasten them on a spit. Then glaze them all over with egg, and sprinkle them with bread-crumbs. Spread on some of the clarified butter, and then another coat of crumbs. Roast them before a clear fire, at least a quarter of an hour. Have ready some nice veal gravy flavoured with lemon-juice, and pour it round the sweet-breads before you send them to table.

LARDED SWEET-BREADS.

Parboil three or four of the largest sweet-breads you can get. This should be done as soon as they are brought in, as few things spoil more rapidly if not cooked at once. When half boiled, lay them in cold water. Prepare a force-meat of grated bread, lemon-peel, butter, salt, pepper, and nutmeg mixed with beaten yolk of egg. Cut open the sweet-breads and stuff them with it, fastening them afterwards with a skewer, or tying them round with packthread. Have ready some slips of bacon-fat, and some slips of lemon-peel cut about the thickness of very small straws. Lard the sweet-breads with them in alternate rows of bacon and lemon-peel, drawing them through with a larding-needle. Do it regularly and handsomely. Then put the sweet-breads into a Dutch oven, and bake them brown. Serve them up with veal gravy flavoured with a glass of Madeira, and enriched with beaten yolk of egg stirred in at the last.

MARBLED VEAL.

Having boiled and skinned two fine smoked tongues, cut them to pieces and pound them to a paste in a mortar, moistening them with plenty of butter as you proceed. Have ready an equal quantity of the lean of veal stewed and cut into very small pieces. Pound the veal also in a mortar, adding butter to it by degrees. The tongue and veal must be kept separate till both have been pounded. Then fill your potting cans with lumps of the veal and tongue, pressed down hard, and so placed, that when cut, the mixture will look variegated or marbled. Close the cans with veal; again press it down very hard, and finish by pouring on clarified butter. Cover the cans closely, and keep them in a dry place. It maybe eaten at tea or supper. Send it to table cut in slices.

You may use it for sandwiches.

MUTTON AND LAMB.

GENERAL REMARKS.

The fore-quarter of a sheep contains the neck, breast, and shoulder; and the hind-quarter the loin and leg. The two loins together are called the chine or saddle. The flesh of good mutton is of a bright red, and a close grain, and the fat firm and quite white. The meat will feel tender and springy when you squeeze it with your fingers. The vein in the neck of the fore-quarter should be of a fine blue.

Lamb is always roasted; generally a whole quarter at once. In carving lamb, the first thing done is to separate the shoulder from the breast, or the leg from the loin.

If the weather is cold enough to allow it, mutton is more tender after being kept a few days.

TO ROAST MUTTON.

Mutton should be roasted with a quick brisk fire. Every part should be trimmed off that cannot be eaten. Wash the meat well. The skin should be taken off and skewered on again before the meat is put on the spit; this will make it more juicy. Otherwise tie paper over the fat, having soaked the twine in water to prevent the string from burning. Put a little salt and water into the dripping-pan, to baste the meat at first, then use its own gravy for that purpose. A quarter of an hour before you think it will be done, take off the skin or paper, dredge the meat very lightly with flour, and baste it with butter. Skim the gravy and send it to table in a boat. A leg of mutton will require from two hours roasting to two hours and a half in proportion to its size. A chine or saddle, from two hours and a half, to three hours. A shoulder, from an hour and a half, to two hours. A loin, from an hour and three quarters, to two hours. A haunch (that is a leg with, part of the loin) cannot be well roasted in less than four hours.

Always have some currant jelly on the table to eat with roast mutton. It should also be accompanied by mashed turnips.

Slices cut from a cold leg of mutton that has been under-done, are very nice broiled or warmed on a gridiron, and sent to the breakfast table covered with currant jelly.

Pickles are always eaten with mutton.

In preparing a leg of mutton for roasting, you may make deep incisions in it, and stuff them with chopped oysters, or with a force-meat made in the usual manner; or with chestnuts parboiled and peeled. The gravy will be improved by stirring into it a glass of port wine.

TO BOIL MUTTON.

To prepare a leg of mutton for boiling, wash it clean, cut a small piece off the shank bone, and trim the knuckle. Put it into a pot with water enough to cover it, and boil it gently for three hours, skimming it well. Then take it from the fire, and keeping the pot well covered, let it finish by remaining in the steam for ten or fifteen minutes. Serve it up with a sauce-boat of melted butter into which a tea-cup full of capers or nasturtians have been stirred.

Have mashed turnips to eat with it.

A few small onions boiled in the water with the mutton are thought by some to improve the flavour of the meat. It is much better when sufficient time is allowed to boil or simmer it slowly.

A neck or a loin of mutton will require also about three hours slow boiling. These pieces should on no account be sent to table the least under-done. Serve up with them carrots and whole turnips. You may add a dish of suet dumplings to eat with the meat, made of finely chopped suet mixed with double its quantity of flour, and a little cold water.

MUTTON CHOPS.

Take chops or steaks from a loin of mutton, cut off the bone close to the meat, and trim off the skin, and part of the fat. Beat them to make them tender, and season them with pepper and salt. Make your gridiron hot over a bed of clear bright coals; rub the bars with suet, and lay on the chops. Turn them frequently; and if the fat that falls from them causes a blaze and smoke, remove the gridiron for a moment till it is over. When they are thoroughly done, put them into a warm dish and butter them. Keep them covered till a moment before they are to be eaten.

When the chops have been turned for the last time, you may strew over them some finely minced onion moistened with boiling water, and seasoned with pepper.

Some like them flavoured with mushroom catchup.

Another way of dressing mutton chops is, after trimming them nicely and seasoning them with pepper and salt, to lay them for awhile in melted butter. When they have imbibed a sufficient quantity, take them out, and cover them all over with grated bread-crumbs. Broil them over a clear fire, and see that the bread does not burn.

CUTLETS À LA MAINTENON.

Cut a neck of mutton into steaks with a bone in each; trim them nicely, and scrape clean the end of the bone. Flatten them with a rolling pin, or a meat beetle, and lay them in oiled butter. Make a seasoning of hard-boiled yolk of egg and sweet-herbs minced small, grated bread, pepper, salt, and nutmeg; and, if you choose, a little minced onion. Take the chops out of the butter, and cover them with the seasoning. Butter some half sheets of white paper, and put the cutlets into them, so as to be entirely covered, securing the paper with pins or strings; and twisting them nicely round the bone. Heat your gridiron over some bright lively coals. Lay the cutlets on it, and broil them about twenty minutes. The custom of sending them to table in the papers had best be omitted, as (unless managed by a French cook) these envelopes, after being on the gridiron, make a very bad appearance.

Serve them up hot, with mushroom sauce in a boat, or with a brown gravy, flavoured with red wine. You may make the gravy of the bones and trimmings, stewed in a little water, skimmed well, and strained when sufficiently stewed. Thicken it with flour browned in a Dutch oven, and add a glass of red wine.

You may bake these cutlets in a Dutch oven without the papers. Moisten them frequently with a little oiled butter.

STEWED MUTTON CHOPS.

Cut a loin or neck of mutton into chops, and trim away the fat and bones. Beat and flatten them. Season them with pepper and salt, and put them into a stew-pan, with barely sufficient water to cover them, and some sliced carrots, turnips, onions, potatoes, and a bunch of sweet herbs, or a few tomatas. Let the whole stew slowly about three hours, or till every thing is tender. Keep the pan closely covered, except when you are skimming it.

Send it to table with sippets or three-cornered pieces of toasted bread, lain all round the dish.

HASHED MUTTON.

Cut into small pieces the lean of some cold mutton that has been under-done, and season it with pepper and salt. Take the bones and other trimmings, put them into a sauce-pan with as much water as will cover them, and some sliced onions, and let them stew till you have drawn from them a good gravy. Having skimmed it well, strain the gravy into a stew-pan, and put the mutton into it. Have ready-boiled some carrots, turnips, potatoes and onions. Slice them, and add them to the meat and gravy. Set the pan on hot coals, and let it simmer till the meat is warmed through, but do not allow it to boil, as it has been once cooked already. Cover the bottom of a dish with slices of buttered toast. Lay the meat and vegetables upon it, and pour over them the gravy.

Tomatas will be found an improvement.

If green peas, or Lima beans are in season, you may boil them, and put them to the hashed mutton; leaving out the other vegetables, or serving them up separately.

A CASSEROLE OF MUTTON.

Butter a deep dish or mould, and line it with potatoes mashed with milk or putter, and seasoned with pepper and salt. Fill it with slices of the lean of cold mutton, or lamb, seasoned also. Cover the whole with more mashed potatoes. Put it into an oven, and bake it till the meat is thoroughly warmed, and the potatoes brown. Then carefully turn it out on a large dish; or you may, if more convenient, send it to table in the dish it was baked in.

MUTTON HARICO.

Take a neck of mutton, cut it into chops, and fry them brown. Then put them into a stew-pan with a bunch of sweet herbs, two or three cloves, a little mace, and pepper and salt to your taste. Cover them with boiling water, and let them stew slowly for about an hour. Then cut some carrots and turnips into dice; slice some onions, and cut up a head of celery; put them all into the stew-pan, and keep it closely covered except when you are skimming off the fat. Let the whole stew gently for an hour longer, and then send it to table in a deep dish, with the gravy about it.

You may make a similar harico of veal steaks, or of beef cut very thin.

STEWED LEG OF MUTTON.

Take a leg of mutton and trim it nicely. Put it into a pot with three pints of water; or with two pints of water and one quart of gravy drawn from bones, trimmings, and coarse pieces of meat. Add some slices of carrots, and a little salt. Stew it slowly three hours. Then put in small onions, small turnips, tomatas or tomata catchup, and shred or powdered sweet marjoram to your taste, and let it stew three hours longer. A large leg will require from first to last from six hours and a half to seven hours stewing. But though it must be tender and well done all through, do not allow it to stew to rags. Serve it up with the vegetables and gravy round it. Have mashed potatoes in another dish.

TO ROAST LAMB.

The best way of cooking lamb is to roast it; when drest otherwise it is insipid, and not so good as mutton. A hind-quarter of eight pounds will be done in about two hours; a fore-quarter of ten pounds, in two hours and a half; a leg of five pounds will take from an hour and a quarter to an hour and a half; a loin about an hour and a half. Lamb, like veal and pork, is not eatable unless thoroughly done; no one preferring it rare, as is frequently the case with beef and mutton.

Wash the meat, wipe it dry, spit it, and cover the fat with paper. Place it before a clear brisk fire. Baste it at first with a little salt and water, and then with its own drippings. Remove the paper when the meat is nearly done, and dredge the lamb with a little flour. Afterwards baste it with butter. Do not take it off the spit till you see it drop white gravy.

Prepare some mint sauce by stripping from the stalks the leaves of young green mint, mincing them very fine, and mixing them with vinegar and sugar. There must be just sufficient vinegar to moisten the mint, but not enough to make the sauce liquid. Send it to table in a boat, and the gravy in another boat. Garnish with sliced lemon.

In carving a quarter of lamb, separate the shoulder from the breast, or the leg from the ribs, sprinkle a little salt and pepper, and squeeze on some lemon juice.

It should be accompanied by asparagus, green peas, and lettuce.

PORK, HAM, ETC.

GENERAL REMARKS.

In cutting up pork, you have the spare-rib, shoulder, griskin or chine, the loin, middlings and leg; the head, feet, heart and liver. On the spare-rib and chine there is but little meat, and the pieces called middlings consist almost entirely of fat. The best parts are the loin, and the leg or hind-quarter. Hogs make the best pork when from two and a half to four years old. They should be kept up and fed with corn at least six weeks before they are killed, or their flesh will acquire a disagreeable taste from the trash and offal which they eat when running at large. The Portuguese pork, which is fed on chestnuts, is perhaps the finest in the world.

If the meat is young, the lean will break on being pinched, and the skin will dent by nipping it with the fingers; the fat will be white, soft, and pulpy. If the skin or rind is rough, and cannot he nipped, it is old.

Hams that have short shank-bones, are generally preferred. If you put a knife under the bone of a ham, and it comes out clean, the meat is good; but quite the contrary if the knife appears smeared and slimy. In good bacon the fat is white, and the lean sticks close to the bone; if it is streaked with yellow, the meat is rusty, and unfit to eat.

Pork in every form should be thoroughly cooked. If the least under-done, it is disgusting and unwholesome.

TO ROAST A PIG.

Begin your preparations by making the stuffing. Take a sufficient quantity of grated stale bread, and mix it with sage and sweet marjoram rubbed fine or powdered; also some grated lemon-peel. Season it with pepper, salt, powdered nutmeg and mace; mix in butter enough to moisten it, and some beaten yolk of egg to bind it. Let the whole be very well incorporated.

The pig should be newly killed, (that morning if possible,) nicely cleaned, fat, and not too large. Wash it well in cold water, and cut off the feet close to the joints, leaving some skin all round to fold over the ends. Take out the liver and heart, and reserve them, with the feet, to make the gravy. Truss back the legs. Fill the body with the stuffing (it must be quite full) and then sew it up, or tie it round with a buttered twine. Put the pig on the spit, and place it before a clear brisk fire, but not too near lest it scorch. The fire should be largest at the ends, that the middle of the pig may not be done before the extremities. If you find the heat too great in the centre, you may diminish it by placing a flat-iron before the fire. When you first put it down, wash the pig all over with salt and water; afterwards rub it frequently with a feather dipped in sweet oil, or with fresh butter tied in a rag. If you baste it with any thing else, or with its own dripping, the skin will not be crisp. Take care not to blister or burn the outside by keeping it too near the fire. A good sized pig will require at least three hours' roasting.

Unless a pig is very small it is seldom sent to table whole. Take the spit from the fire, and place it across a large dish: then, having cut off the head with a sharp knife, and cut down the back, slip the spit out. Lay the two halves of the body close together in the dish, and place half the head on each side. Garnish with sliced lemon.

For the gravy,—take, that from the dripping-pan and skim it well. Having boiled the heart, liver, and feet, with some minced sage in a very little water, cut the meat from the feet, and chop it. Chop also the liver and heart. Put all into a small sauce-pan, adding a little of the water that they were boiled in, and some bits of butter rolled in flour. Flavour it with a glass of Madeira, and some grated nutmeg. Give it a boil up, and send it to table in a gravy-boat.

You may serve up with the pig, apple-sauce, cranberry sauce, or bread-sauce in a small tureen; or currant jelly.

If you bake the pig instead of roasting it, rub it from time to time with fresh butter tied in a rag.

TO ROAST A LEG OF PORK.

Take a sharp knife and score the skin across in narrow stripes (you may cross it again so as to form diamonds) and rub in some powdered sage. Raise the skin at the knuckle, and put in a stuffing of minced onion and sage, bread-crumbs, pepper, salt, and beaten yolk of egg. Fasten it down with a buttered string, or with skewers. You may make deep incisions in the meat of the large end of the leg, and stuff them also; pressing in the filling very hard. Rub a little sweet oil all over the skin with a brush or a goose feather, to make it crisp and of a handsome brown. Do not place the spit too near the fire, lest the skin should burn and blister. A leg of pork will require from three to four hours to roast. Moisten it all the time by brushing it with sweet oil, or with fresh butter tied in a rag. To baste it with its own dripping will make the skin tough and hard. Skim the fat carefully from the gravy, which should be thickened with a little flour.

A roast leg of pork should always be accompanied by apple-sauce, and by mashed potato and mashed turnips.

TO ROAST A LOIN OF PORK.

Score the skin in narrow strips, and rub it all over with a mixture of powdered sage leaves, pepper and salt. Have ready a force-meat or stuffing of minced onions and sage, mixed with a little grated bread and beaten yolk of egg, and seasoned with pepper and salt. Make deep incisions between the ribs and fill them with this stuffing. Put it on the spit before a clear fire and moisten it with butter or sweet oil, rubbed lightly over it. It will require three hours to roast.

Having skimmed the gravy well, thicken it with a little flour, and serve it up in a boat. Have ready some apple-sauce to eat with the pork. Also mashed turnips and mashed potatoes.

You may roast in the same manner, a shoulder, spare-rib, or chine of pork; seasoning it with sage and onion.

TO ROAST A MIDDLING OR SPRING PIECE OF PORK.

Make a force-meat of grated bread, and minced onion and sage, pepper, salt, and beaten yolk of egg; mix it well, and spread it all over the inside of the pork. Then roll up the meat, and with a sharp knife score it round in circles, rubbing powdered sage into the cuts. Tie a buttered twine round the roll of meat so as to keep it together in every direction. Put a hook through one end, and roast the pork before a clear brisk fire, moistening the skin occasionally with butter. Or you may bake it in a Dutch oven. It is a good side dish. Thicken the gravy with a little flour, and flavour it with a glass of wine. Have currant jelly to eat with it.

It should be delicate young pork.

TO STEW PORK.

Take a nice piece of the fillet or leg of fresh pork; rub it with a little salt, and score the skin. Put it into a pot with sufficient water to cover it, and stew it gently for two hours or more, in proportion to its size. Then put into the same pot a dozen or more sweet potatoes, scraped, split, and cut in pieces. Let the whole stew gently together for an hour and a half, or till all is thoroughly done, skimming it frequently. Serve up all together in a large dish.

This stew will be found very good. For sweet potatoes you may substitute white ones mixed with sliced turnips, or parsnips scraped or split.

TO BOIL CORNED PORK.

Take a nice piece of fresh pork, (the leg is the best,) rub it with salt, and let it lie in the salt two days. Boil it slowly in plenty of water, skimming it well. When the meat is about half done, you may put into the same pot a fine cabbage, washed clean and quartered. The pork and the cabbage should be thoroughly done, and tender throughout. Send them to table in separate dishes, having drained and squeezed all the water out of the cabbage. Take off the skin of the pork, and touch the outside at intervals with spots of cayenne pepper. Eat mustard with it.

Pork is never boiled unless corned or salted.

PICKLED PORK AND PEASE PUDDING.

Soak the pork all night in cold water, and wash and scrape it clean. Put it on early in the day, as it will take a long time to boil, and must boil slowly. Skim it frequently. Boil in a separate pot greens or cabbage to eat with it; also parsnips and potatoes.

Pease pudding is a frequent accompaniment to pickled pork, and is very generally liked. To make a small pudding, you must have ready a quart of dried split pease, which have been soaked all night in cold water. Tie them in a cloth, (leaving room for them to swell,) and boil them slowly till they are tender. Drain them, and rub them through a cullender or a sieve into a deep dish; season them with pepper and salt, and mix with them an ounce of butter, and two beaten eggs. Beat all well together till thoroughly mixed. Dip a clean cloth in hot water, sprinkle it with flour, and put the pudding into it. Tie it up very tightly, leaving a small space between the mixture and the tying, (as the pudding will still swell a little,) and boil it an hour longer. Send it to table and eat it with the pork.

You may make a pease pudding in a plain and less delicate way, by simply seasoning the pease with pepper and salt, (having first soaked them well,) tying them in a cloth, and putting them to boil in the same pot with the pork, taking care to make the string very tight, so that the water may not get in. When all is done, and you turn out the pudding, cut it into thick slices and lay it round the pork.

Pickled pork is frequently accompanied by dried beans and hominy.

PORK AND BEANS.

Allow two pounds of pickled pork to two quarts of dried beans. If the meat is very salt put it in soak over night. Put the beans into a pot with cold water, and let them hang all night over the embers of the fire, or set them in the chimney corner, that they may warm as well as soak. Early in the morning rinse them through a cullender. Score the rind of the pork, (which should not be a very fat piece,) and put the meat into a clean pot with the beans, which must be seasoned with pepper. Let them boil slowly together for about two hours, and carefully remove all the scum and fat that rises to the top. Then take them out; lay the pork in a tin pan, and cover the meat with the beans, adding a very little water. Put it into an oven, and bake it four hours.

This is a homely dish, but is by many persons much liked. It is customary to bring it to table in the pan in which it is baked.

PORK STEAKS.

Pork steaks or chops should be taken from the neck, or the loin. Cut them about half an inch thick, remove the skin, trim them neatly, and beat them. Season them with pepper, salt, and powdered sage-leaves or sweet marjoram, and broil them over a clear fire till quite done all through, turning them once. They require much longer broiling than beef-steaks of mutton chops. When you think they are nearly done, take up one on a plate and try it. If it is the least red inside, return it to the gridiron. Have ready a gravy made of the trimmings, or any coarse pieces of pork stewed in a little water with chopped onions and sage, and skimmed carefully. When all the essence is extracted, take out the bits of meat, &c., and serve up the gravy in a boat to eat with the steaks.

They should be accompanied with apple-sauce.

PORK CUTLETS.

Cut them from the leg, and remove the skin; trim them and beat them, and sprinkle on salt and pepper. Prepare some beaten egg in a pan; and on a flat dish a mixture of bread-crumbs, minced onion, and sage. Put some lard or drippings into a frying-pan over the fire; and when it boils, put in the cutlets; having dipped every one first in the egg, and then in the seasoning. Fry them twenty or thirty minutes, turning them often. After you have taken them out of the frying-pan, skim the gravy, dredge in a little flour, give it one boil, and then pour it on the dish round the cutlets.

Have apple-sauce to eat with them.

Pork cutlets prepared in this manner may be stewed instead of being fried. Add to them a little water, and stew them slowly till thoroughly done, keeping them closely covered except when you remove the lid to skim them.

PORK PIE.

Take the lean of a leg or loin of fresh pork, and season it with pepper, salt, and nutmeg. Cover the bottom and sides of a deep dish, with, a good paste, made with a pound of butter to two pounds of flour, and rolled out thick. Put in a layer of pork, and then a layer of pippin apples, pared, cored, and cut small. Strew over the apples sufficient sugar to make them very sweet. Then place another layer of pork, and so on till the dish is full. Pour in half a pint or more of water, or of white wine. Cover the pie with a thick lid of paste, and notch and ornament it according to your taste.

Set it in a brisk oven, and bake it well.

HAM PIE.

Cover the sides and bottom of a dish with a good pasts rolled out thick. Have ready some slices of cold boiled ham, about half an inch thick, some eggs boiled hard and sliced, and a large young fowl cleaned and Cut up. Put a layer of ham at the bottom, then the fowl, then the eggs, and then another layer of ham. Shake on some pepper, and pour in some water, or what will be much better, some veal gravy. Cover the pie with a crust, notch and ornament it, and bake it well.

Some mushrooms will greatly improve it.

Small button mushrooms will keep very well in a bottle of sweet oil—first peeling the skin, and cutting off the stalks.

HAM SANDWICHES

Cut some thin slices of bread very neatly, having slightly buttered them; and, if you choose, spread on a very little mustard. Have ready some very thin slices of cold boiled ham, and lay one between two slices of bread. You may either roll them up, or lay them flat on the plates. They are used at supper, or at luncheon.

You may substitute for the ham, cold smoked tongue, shred or grated.

BROILED HAM.

Cut the ham into very thin slices, (the thinner the better.) Soak them in hot water at least half an hour, (a whole hour is better,) to draw out some of the salt; changing the water several times, and always pouring it on scalding hot. This process will not only extract the superfluous salt (which would otherwise ooze out in broiling and remain sticking about the surface of the meat) but it makes the ham more tender and mellow. After soaking, dry the slices in a cloth, and then heat your gridiron, and broil them over a clear fire.

If you have cold boiled ham, it is better for broiling than that which is raw; and being boiled, will require no soaking before you put it on the gridiron.

If you wish to serve up eggs with the ham, put some lard into a very clean frying-pan, and make it boiling hot. Break the eggs separately into a saucer, that in case a bad one should be among them it may not mix with the rest. Slip each egg gently into the frying-pan. Do not turn them while they are frying, but keep pouring some of the hot lard over them with an iron spoon; this will do them sufficiently on the upper side. They will be done enough in about three minutes; the white must retain its transparency so that the yolk will be seen through it. When done, take them up with a tin slice, drain off the lard, and if any part of the white is discoloured or ragged, trim it off. Lay a fried egg upon each slice of the broiled ham, and send them to table hot.

This is a much nicer way than the common practice of frying the ham or bacon with the eggs. Some persons broil or fry the ham without eggs, and send it to table cut into little slips or mouthfuls.

To curl small pieces of ham for garnishing, slice as thin as possible some that has been boiled or parboiled. The pieces should be about two inches square. Roll it up round little wooden skewers, and put it into a cheese toaster, or into a tin oven, and set it before the fire for eight or ten minutes. When it is done, slip out the skewers.

TO BOIL A HAM.

Hams should always be soaked in water previous to boiling, to draw out a portion of the salt, and to make them tender. They will soften more easily if soaked in lukewarm water. If it is a new ham, and not very salt or hard, you need not put it in water till the evening before you intend to cook it. An older one will require twenty-four hours' soaking; and one that is very old and hard should be kept in soak two or three days, frequently changing the water, which must be soft. Soak it in a tub, and keep it well covered. When you take it out of the water to prepare it for boiling, scrape and trim it nicely, and pare off all the bad looking parts.

Early in the morning put it into a large pot or kettle with plenty of cold water. Place it over a slow fire that it may heat gradually; it should not come to a boil in less than an hour and a half, or two hours. When it boils, quicken the fire, and skim the pot carefully. Then simmer it gently four or fire hours or more, according to its size. A ham weighing fifteen pounds should simmer five hours after it has come to a boil. Keep the pot well skimmed.

When it is done, take it up, carefully strip off the skin, and reserve it to cover the ham when it is put away cold. Rub the ham all over with some beaten egg, and strew on it fine bread-raspings shaken through the lid of a dredging box. Then place it in an oven to brown and crisp, or on a hot dish set over the pot before the fire. Cut some writing paper into a handsome fringe, and twist it round the shank-bone before you send the ham to table. Garnish the edge of the dish with little piles or spots of rasped crust of bread.

In carving a ham, begin not quite in the centre, but a little nearer to the hock. Cut the slices very thin. It is not only a most ungenteel practice to cut ham in thick slices, but it much impairs the flavour.

When you put it away after dinner, skewer on again the skin. This will make it keep the better.

Ham should always be accompanied by green vegetables, such as asparagus, peas, beans, spinach, cauliflower, brocoli, &c.

Bacon also should be well soaked before it is cooked; and it should be boiled very slowly, and for a long time. The greens may be boiled with the meat. Take care to skim the pot carefully, and to drain and squeeze the greens very well before you send them to table. If there are yellow streaks in the lean of the bacon, it is rusty, and unfit to eat.

TO ROAST A HAM.

Take a very fine ham (a Westphalia one if you can procure it) and soak it in lukewarm water for a day or two, changing the water frequently. The day before you intend cooking it, take the ham out of the water, and (having removed the skin) trim it nicely, and pour over it a bottle of Madeira or sherry. Let it steep till next morning, frequently during the day washing the wine over it. Put it on the spit in time to allow at least six hours for slowly roasting it. Baste it continually with hot water. When it is done, dredge it all over with fine bread-raspings shaken on through the top of the dredging box; and set it before the fire to brown.

For gravy, take the wine in which the ham was steeped, and add to it the essence or juice which flowed from the meat when taken from the spit.

Squeeze in the juice of two lemons. Put it into a sauce-pan, and boil and skim it. Send it to table in a boat. Cover the shank of the ham (which should have been sawed short) with bunches of double parsley, and ornament it with a cluster of flowers cut out with a penknife from raw carrots, beets, and turnips; and made to imitate marygolds, and red and white roses.

DIRECTIONS FOR CURING HAM OR BACON.

Ham or bacon, however well cured, will never be good unless the pork of which it is made has been properly fed. The hogs should be well fattened on corn, and fed with it about eight weeks, allowing ten bushels to each hog. They are best for curing when from two to four years old, and should not weigh more than one hundred and fifty or one hundred and sixty pounds. The first four weeks they may be fed on mush, or on Indian meal moistened with water; the remaining four on corn unground; giving them always as much as they will eat. Soap-suds may be given to them three or four times a week; or oftener if convenient.

When killed and cut up, begin immediately to salt them. Rub the outside of each ham with a tea-spoonful of powdered saltpetre, and the inside with a tea-spoonful of cayenne pepper. Having mixed together brown sugar and fine salt, in the proportion of a pound and a half of brown sugar to a quart of salt, rub the pork well with it. This quantity of sugar and salt will be sufficient for fifty pounds of meat. Have ready some large tubs, the bottoms sprinkled with salt, and lay the meat in the tubs with the skin downward. Put plenty of salt between each layer of meat. After it has lain eight days, take it out and wipe off all the salt, and wash the tubs. Make a pickle of soft water, equal quantities of salt and molasses, and a little saltpetre; allowing four ounces of saltpetre to two quarts of molasses and two quarts of salt, which is the proportion for fifty pounds of meat. The pickle must be strong enough to bear up an egg. Boil and skim it; and when it is cold, pour it over the meat, which must be turned every day and basted with the pickle. The hams should remain in the pickle at least four weeks; the shoulders and middlings of the bacon three weeks; and the jowls two weeks. They should then be taken out and smoked. Having washed off the pickle, before you smoke the meat, bury it, while wet, in a tub of bran. This will form a crust over it, and prevent evaporation of the juices. Let the smoke-house be ready to receive the meat immediately. Take it out of the tub after it has lain half an hour, and rub the bran evenly over it. Then hang it up to smoke with the small end downwards. The smoke-house should be dark and cool, and should stand alone, for the heat occasioned by an adjoining—building may spoil the meat, or produce insects. Keep up a good smoke all day, but have no blaze. Hickory is the best wood for a smoke-house fire, In three or four weeks the meat will be sufficiently smoked, and fit for use. During the process it should be occasionally taken down, examined, and hung up again. The best way of keeping hams is to wrap them in paper, or, to sew them in coarse cloths (which should be white-washed) and bury them in a barrel of hickory ashes. The ashes must be frequently changed.

An old ham will require longer to soak, and longer to boil than a new one.

Tongues may be cured in the above manner.

LIVER PUDDINGS.

Boil some pigs' livers. When cold, mince them, and season them with pepper, salt, and some sage and sweet marjoram rubbed fine. You may add some powdered cloves. Have ready some large skins nicely cleaned, and fill them with the mixture, tying up the ends securely. Prick them with a fork to prevent their bursting; put them into hot water, and boil them slowly for about an hour. They will require no farther cooking before you eat them. Keep them in stone jars closely covered. They are eaten cold at breakfast or supper, cut into slices an inch thick or more; or they may be cut into large pieces, and broiled or fried.

COMMON SAUSAGE-MEAT.

Having cleared it from the skin, sinews, and gristle, take six pounds of the lean of young fresh pork, and three pounds of the fat, and mince it all as fine as possible. Take some dried sage, pick off the leaves and rub them to powder, allowing three tea-spoonfuls to each pound of meat. Having mixed the fat and lean well together, and seasoned it with nine tea-spoonfuls of pepper, and the same quantity of salt, strew on the powdered sage, and mix the whole very well with your hands. Put it away in a stone jar, packing it down hard; and keep it closely covered. Set the jar in a cool dry place.

When you wish to use the sausage-meat, make it into flat cakes about an inch thick and the size of a dollar; dredge them with flour, and fry them in butter or dripping, over rather a slow fire, till they are well browned on both sides, and thoroughly done.

Sausages are seldom eaten except at breakfast.

FINE SAUSAGES.

Take some fresh pork, (the leg is best,) and clear it from the skin, sinews, and gristle. Allow two pounds of fat to three pounds of lean. Mince it all very fine, and season it with two ounces and a half of salt, half an ounce of pepper, thirty cloves, and a dozen blades of mace powdered, three grated, nutmegs, six table-spoonfuls of powdered sage, and two tea-spoonfuls of powdered rosemary. Mix all well together. Put it into a stone jar, and press it down very hard. Cover it closely, and keep it in a dry cool place.

When you use this sausage-meat, mix with it some beaten yolk of egg, and make it into balls or cakes. Dredge them with flour, and fry them in butter.

BOLOGNA SAUSAGES.

Take ten pounds of beef, and four pounds of pork; two-thirds of the meat should be lean, and only one third fat. Chop it very fine, and mix it well together. Then season it with six ounces of fine salt, one ounce of black pepper, half an ounce of cayenne, one table-spoonful of powdered cloves; and one clove or garlic minced very fine.

Have ready some large skins nicely cleaned and prepared, (they should be beef-skins,) and wash them in salt and vinegar. Fill them with the above mixture, and secure the ends by tying them with packthread or fine twine. Make a brine of salt and water strong enough to bear up an egg. Put the sausages into it, and let them lie for three weeks, turning them daily. Then take them out, wipe them dry, hang them up and smoke them. Before you put them away rub them all over with, sweet oil,

Keep them in ashes. That of vine-twigs is best for them.

You may fry them or not before you eat them.

PORK CHEESE.

Take the heads, tongues, and feet of young fresh pork, or any other pieces that are convenient. Having removed the skin, boil them till all the meat is quite tender, and can be easily stripped from the bones. Then chop it small, and season it with salt and black pepper to your taste, and if you choose, some beaten cloves. Add sage-leaves and sweet marjoram, minced fine, or rubbed to powder. Mix the whole very well together with your hands. Put it into deep pans, with straight sides, (the shape of a cheese,) press it down hard and closely with a plate that will fit the pan; putting the under side of the plate next to the meat, and placing a heavy weight on it. In two or three days it will be fit for use, and you may turn it out of the pan. Send it to table cut in slices, and use mustard and vinegar with it. It is generally eaten at supper or breakfast.

PIG'S FEET AND EARS SOUSED.

Having cleaned them properly, and removed the skin, boil them slowly till they are quite tender, and then split the feet and put them with the ears into salt and vinegar, flavoured with a little mace. Cover the jar closely, and set it away. When you use them, dry each piece well with a cloth; dip them first in beaten yolk of egg, and then in bread-crumbs, and fry them nicely in butter or lard. Or you may eat them cold, just out of the vinegar.

If you intend keeping them some time, you must make a fresh pickle for them every other day.

TO IMITATE WESTPHALIA HAM.

The very finest pork must be used for these hams. Mix together an equal quantity of powdered saltpetre and brown sugar, and rub it well into the hams. Next day make a pickle in sufficient quantity to cover them very well. The proportions of the ingredients are a pound and a half of fine salt, half a pound of brown sugar, an ounce of black pepper and an ounce of cloves pounded to powder, a small bit of sal prunella, and a quart of stale strong beer or porter. Boil them all together, so as to make a pickle that will bear up an egg. Pour it boiling hot over the meat, and let it lie in the pickle two weeks, turning it two or three times every day, and basting or washing it with the liquid. Then take out the hams, rub them with bran and smoke them for a fortnight. When done, keep them in a barrel of wood ashes.

In cooking these hams simmer them slowly for seven or eight hours.

To imitate the shape of the real Westphalia hams, cut some of the meat off the under side of the thick part, so as to give them a flat appearance. Do this before you begin to cure them, first loosening the skin and afterwards sewing it on again.

The ashes in which you keep them must be changed frequently, wiping the hams when you take them out.

TO GLAZE A COLD HAM.

With a brush or quill feather go all over the ham with beaten yolk of egg. Then cover it thickly with pounded cracker, made as fine as flour, or with grated crumbs of stale bread. Lastly go over it with thick cream. Put it to brown in the oven of a stove, or brown it on the spit of a tin roaster, set before the fire and turned frequently.

This glazing will be found delicious.

VENISON, ETC.

TO ROAST A SADDLE OR HAUNCH OF VENISON.

Wipe it all over with a sponge dipped in warm water Then rub the skin with lard or nice dripping. Cover the fat with sheets of paper two double, buttered, and tied on with packthread that has been soaked to keep it from burning. Or, what is still better, you may cover the first sheets of paper with a coarse paste of flour and water rolled out half an inch thick, and then cover the paste with the second sheets of paper, securing the whole well with the string to prevent its falling off. Place the venison on the spit before a strong clear fire, such as you would have for a sirloin of beef, and let the fire be well kept up all the time. Put some claret and butter into the dripping-pan and baste the meat with it frequently. If wrapped in paste, it will not be done in less than five hours. Half an hour before you take it up, remove the coverings carefully, place the meat nearer to the fire, baste it with fresh butter and dredge it very lightly with flour. Send it to table with fringed white paper wrapped round the bone, and its own gravy well skimmed. Have currant jelly to eat with it. As venison chills immediately, the plates should be kept on heaters.

You may make another gravy with a pound and a half of scraps and trimmings or inferior pieces of venison, put into a sauce-pan with three pints of water, a few cloves, a few blades of mace, half a nutmeg; and salt and cayenne to your taste. Boil it down slowly to a pint. Then skim off the fat, and strain the gravy into a clean sauce-pan. Add to it half a pint of currant jelly, half a pint of claret, and near a quarter of a pound of butter divided into bits and rolled in flour. Send it to table in two small tureens or sauce-boats. This gravy will be found very fine.

Venison should never be roasted unless very fat. The shoulder is a roasting piece, and may be done without the paper or paste.

Venison is best when quite fresh; but if it is expedient to keep it a week before you cook it, wash it well with milk and water, and then dry it perfectly with cloths till there is not the least damp remaining on it. Then mix together powdered ginger and pepper, and rub it well over every part of the meat. Do not, however, attempt to keep it unless the weather is quite cold.

TO HASH COLD VENISON.

Cut the meat in nice small slices, and put the trimmings and bones into a sauce-pan with barely water enough to cover them. Let them stew for an hour. Then strain the liquid into a stew-pan; add to it some bits of butter rolled in flour, and whatever gravy was left of the venison the day before. Stir in some currant jelly, and give it a boil up. Then put in the meat, and keep it over the fire just long enough to warm it through; but do not allow it to boil, as it has been once cooked already.

VENISON STEAKS.

Cut them from the neck or haunch. Season them with pepper and salt. When the gridiron has been well heated over a bed of bright coals, grease the bars, and lay the steaks upon it. Broil them well, turning them once, and taking care to save as much of the gravy as possible. Serve them up with some currant jelly laid on each steak. Have your plates set on heaters.

VENISON PASTY.

The neck, breast, and shoulder are the parts used for a venison pie or pasty. Cut the meat into pieces (fat and lean together) and put the bones and trimmings into a stew-pan with pepper and salt, and water or veal broth enough to cover it. Simmer it till you have drawn out a good gravy. Then strain it.

In the mean time make a good rich paste, and roll it rather thick. Cover the bottom and sides of a deep dish with one sheet of it, and put in your meat, having seasoned it with pepper, salt, nutmeg, and mace. Pour in the gravy which you have prepared from the trimmings, and two glasses of port or claret, and lay on the top some hits of butter rolled in flour. Cover the pie with a thick lid of paste, and ornament it handsomely with leaves and flowers formed with a tin cutter. Bake it two hours or more, according to its size.

VENISON HAMS.

Venison for hams must be newly killed, and in every respect as good as possible. Mix together equal quantities of salt and brown sugar, and rub it well into the hams. Put them into a tub, and let them lie seven days; turning them and rubbing them daily with the mixture of salt and sugar. Next mix together saltpetre and common salt, in the proportion of two ounces of saltpetre to a handful of salt. Rub it well into your hams, and let them lie a week longer. Then wipe them, rub them with bran, and smoke them a fortnight over hickory wood. Pack them in wood ashes.

Venison ham must not be cooked before it is eaten. It is used for the tea-table, chipped or shred like dried beef, to which it is considered very superior.

It will not keep as long as other smoked meat.

TO ROAST A KID.

A kid should be cooked the day it is killed, or the day after at farthest. They are best from three to four months old, and are only eaten while they live on milk.

Wash the kid well, wipe it dry, and truss it. Stuff the body with a force-meat of grated bread, butter or suet, sweet herbs, pepper, salt, nutmeg, grated lemon-peel, and beaten egg; and sew it up to keep the stuffing in its place. Put it on the spit and rub it over with lard, or sweet oil. Put a little salt and water into the dripping-pan, and baste the kid first with that, and afterwards with its own gravy. Or you may make it very nice by basting it with cream. It should roast about three hours. At the last, transfer the gravy to a small sauce-pan; thicken it with a little butter rolled in flour, give it a boil up, and send it to table in a boat. Garnish the kid with lumps of currant jelly laid round the edge of the dish.

A fawn (which should never be kept more than one day) may be roasted in the same manner; also, a hare, or a couple of rabbits.

You may send to table, to eat with the kid, a dish of chestnuts boiled or roasted, and divested of the shells.

TO ROAST A HARE.

If a hare is old do not roast it, but make soup of it. Wash and soak it in water for an hour, and change the water several times, having made a little slit in the neck to let out the blood. Take out the heart and liver, and scald them. Drain, dry, and truss the hare. Make a force-meat richer and more moist than usual, and add to it the heart and liver minced fine. Soak the bread-crumbs in a little claret before you mix them with the other ingredients. Stuff the body of the hare with this force-meat, and sew it up. Put it on the spit, rub it with butter, and roast it before a brisk fire. For the first half hour baste it with butter; and afterwards with cream, or with milk thickened with beaten yolk of egg. At the last, dredge it lightly with flour. The hare will require about two hours roasting.

For sauce, take the drippings of the hare mixed with cream or with claret, and a little lemon-juice, a bit of butter, and some bread-crumbs. Give it a boil up, and send it to table in a boat. Garnish the hare with slices of currant jelly laid round it in the dish.

FRICASSEED RABBITS.

The best way of cooking rabbits is to fricassee them. Take a couple of fine ones, and cut them up, or disjoint them. Put them into a stew-pan; season them with cayenne pepper and salt, some chopped parsley, and some powdered mace. Pour in a pint of warm water (or of veal broth, if you have it) and stew it over a slow fire till the rabbits are quite tender; adding (when they are about half done) some bits of butter rolled in flour. Just before you take it from the fire, enrich the gravy with a jill or more of thick cream with some nutmeg grated into it. Stir the gravy well, but take care not to let it boil after the cream is in, lest it curdle.

Put the pieces of rabbit on a hot dish, and pour the gravy over them.

POULTRY, GAME, ETC.

GENERAL REMARKS

In buying poultry choose those that are fresh and fat. Half-grown poultry is comparatively insipid; it is best when full-grown but not old. Old poultry is tough and hard. An old goose is so tough as to be frequently uneatable. When poultry is young the skin is thin and tender, and can be easily tipped by trying it with a pin; the legs are smooth; the feet moist and limber; and the eyes full and bright. The body should be thick and the breast fat. The bill and feet of a young goose are yellow, and have but few hairs on them; when old they are red and hairy.

Poultry is best when killed overnight, as if cooked too soon after-killing, it is hard and does not taste well. It is not the custom in America, as in some parts of Europe, to keep game, or indeed any sort of eatable, till it begins to taint; all food when inclining to decomposition being regarded by us with disgust.

When poultry or game is frozen, it should be brought into the kitchen early in the morning of the day on which it is to be cooked. It may be thawed by laying it several hours in cold water. If it is not thawed it will require double the time to cook, and will be tough and tasteless when done. In drawing poultry be very careful not to break the gall, lest its disagreeable bitterness should be communicated to the liver.

Poultry should be always scalded in hot water to make the feathers come out easily. Before they are cooked they should be held for a moment over the blaze of the fire to singe off the hairs that are about the skin. The head, neck, and feet should be cut off, and the ends of the legs skewered in the bodies. A string should be tied tightly round.

TO BOIL A PAIR OF FOWLS.

Make a force-meat in the usual manner, of grated, bread-crumbs, chopped sweet herbs, butter, pepper, salt, and yolk of egg. Fill the bodies of the fowls with the stuffing, and tie a string firmly round them. Skewer the livers and gizzards to the sides, under the wings. Dredge them with flour, and put them into a pot with just enough of water to cook them; cover it closely, and put it over a moderate fire. As soon as the scum rises, take off the pot and skim it. Then cover it again, and boil it slowly half an hour. Afterwards diminish the fire, and let them stew slowly till quite tender. An hour altogether is generally sufficient to boil a pair of fowls, unless they are quite old. By doing them slowly (rather stewing than boiling) the skin will not break, and they will be whiter and more tender than if boiled fast.

Serve them up with egg-sauce in a boat.

Young chickens are better for being soaked two hours in skim milk, previous to boiling. You need not stuff them. Boil or stew them, slowly in the same manner as large fowls. Three quarters of an hour will cook them.

Serve them up with parsley-sauce, and garnish with parsley.

Boiled fowls should be accompanied by ham or smoked tongue.

TO ROAST A PAIR. OF FOWLS.

Leave out the livers, gizzards and hearts, to be chopped and put into the gravy.—Fill the crops and bodies of the fowls with a force-meat, put them before a clear fire and roast them an hour, basting them with butter or with clarified dripping.

Having stewed the necks, gizzards, livers, and hearts in a very little water, strain it and mix it hot with the gravy that has dripped from the fowls, and which must be first skimmed. Thicken it with a little browned flour, add to it the livers, hearts, and gizzards chopped small. Send the fowls to table with the gravy in a boat, and have cranberry-sauce to eat with them.

BROILED CHICKENS.

Split a pair of chickens down the back, and beat them flat, Wipe the inside, season them with pepper and salt, and let them, lie while you prepare some beaten yolk of egg and grated bread-crumbs. Wash the outside of the chickens all over with the egg, and then strew on the bread-crumbs. Have ready a hot gridiron over a bed of bright coals. Lay the chickens on it with the inside downwards, or next the fire. Broil them about three quarters of an hour, keeping them covered with a plate. Just before you take them up, lay some small pieces of butter on them.

In preparing chickens for broiling, you may parboil them about ten minutes, to ensure their being sufficiently cooked; as it is difficult to broil the thick parts thoroughly without burning the rest.

FRICASSEED CHICKENS.

Having cut up your chickens, lay them in cold water till all the blood is drawn out. Then wipe the pieces, season them with pepper and salt, and dredge them with flour. Fry them in lard or butter; they should be of a fine brown on both sides. When they are quite done, take them, out of the frying-pan, cover them up, and set them by the fire to keep warm. Skim the gravy in the frying-pan and pour into it half a pint of cream; season it with a little nutmeg, pepper and salt, and thicken it with, a small bit of butter rolled in flour. Give it a boil, and then pour it round the chickens, which must he kept hot. Put some lard into the pan, and fry some parsley in It to lay on the pieces of chicken; it must be done green and crisp.

To make a white fricassee of chickens, skin them, cut them in pieces, and having soaked out the blood, season them with salt, pepper, nutmeg and mace, and strew over them some sweet marjoram shred fine. Put them into a stew-pan, and pour over them half a pint of cream, or rich unskimmed milk. Add some butter rolled in Hour, and (if you choose) some small force-meat balls. Set the stew-pan over hot coals. Keep it closely covered, and stew or simmer it gently till the chicken is quite tender, but do not allow it to boil.

You may improve it by a few small slices of cold ham.

CHICKEN CROQUETS AND RISSOLES.

Take some cold chicken, and having; cut the flesh from the bones, mince it small with a little suet and parsley; adding sweet marjoram and grated lemon-peel. Season it with pepper, salt and nutmeg, and having mixed the whole very well pound it to a paste in a marble mortar, putting in a little at a time, and moistening it frequently with yolk of egg that has been previously beaten. Then divide it into equal portions and having floured your hands, make it up in the shape of pears, sticking the head of a clove into the bottom of each to represent the blossom end, and the stalk of a clove into the top to look like the stem. Dip them into beaten yolk of egg, and then into bread-crumbs grated finely and sifted. Fry them in butter, and when you take them out of the pan, fry some parsley in it. Having drained the parsley, cover the bottom of a dish with it, and lay the croquets upon it. Send it to table as a side dish.

Croquets maybe made of cold sweet-breads, or of cold veal mixed with ham or tongue.

Rissoles are made of the same ingredients, well mixed, and beaten smooth in a mortar. Make a fine paste, roll it out, and cut it into round cakes. Then lay some of the mixture on one half of the cake, and fold over the other upon it, in the shape of a half-moon. Close and crimp the edges nicely, and fry the rissoles in butter. They should be of a light brown on both sides. Drain them and send them to table dry.

BAKED CHICKEN PIE.

Cover the bottom and sides of a deep dish with a thick paste. Having cut up your chickens, and seasoned them to your taste, with salt, pepper, mace and nutmeg, put them in, and lay on the top several pieces of butter rolled in flour. Fill up the dish about two-thirds with cold water. Then lay on the top crust, notching it handsomely. Cut a slit in the top, and stick into it an ornament of paste made in the form of a tulip. Bake it in a moderate oven.

It will be much improved by the addition of a quarter of a hundred oysters; or by interspersing the pieces of chicken with slices of cold boiled ham.

You may add also some yolks of eggs boiled hard.

A duck pie may be made in the same manner. A rabbit pie also.

A POT PIE.

Take a pair of large fine fowls. Cut them up, wash the pieces, and season them with pepper and salt. Make a good paste in the proportion of a pound and a half of minced suet to three pounds of flour. Let there be plenty of paste, as it is always much liked by the eaters of pot pie. Roll out the paste not very thin, and cut most of it into long squares. Butter the sides of a pot, and line them with paste nearly to the top. Lay slices of cold ham at the bottom of the pot, and then the pieces of fowl, interspersed all through with squares of paste, and potatoes pared and quartered. Lay a lid of paste all over the top, leaving a hole in the middle. Pour in about a quart of water, cover the pot, and boil it slowly but steadily for two hours. Half an hour before you take it up, put in through the hole in the centre of the crust, some bits of butter rolled in flour, to thicken the gravy. When done put the pie on a large dish, and pour the gravy over it.

You may intersperse it all through with cold ham.

A pot pie may be made of ducks, rabbits, squirrels, or venison. Also of beef-steaks.

CHICKEN CURRY.

Take a pair of fine fowls, and having cut them in pieces, lay them in salt and water till the seasoning is ready. Take two table-spoonfuls of powdered ginger, one table-spoonful of fresh turmeric, a tea-spoonful of ground black pepper; some mace, a few cloves, some cardamom seeds, and a little cayenne pepper with a small portion of salt. These last articles according to your taste. Put all into a mortar, and add to them eight large onions, chopped or cut small. Mix and beat all together, till the onions, spices, &c. form a paste.

Put the chickens into a pan with sufficient butter rolled in flour, and fry them till they are brown, but not till quite done. While this is proceeding, set over the fire a sauce-pan three parts full of water, or sufficient to cover the chickens when they are ready. As soon as the water boils, throw in the curry-paste. When the paste has all dissolved, and is thoroughly mixed with the water, put in the pieces of chicken to boil, or rather to simmer. When the chicken is quite done, put it into a large dish, and eat it with boiled rice. The rice may either be laid round on the same dish, or served up separately.

This is a genuine East India receipt for curry.

Lamb, veal, or rabbits may be curried in the same manner.

To boil Rice for the Curry.

Pick the rice carefully, to clear it from husks and motes. Then soak it in cold water for a quarter of an hour, or more. When you are ready to boil it, pour off the water in which it has soaked. Have ready a pot or sauce-pan of boiling water, into which you have put a little salt. Allow two quarts of water to a pound of rice. Sprinkle the rice gradually into the water. Boil it hard for twenty minutes, then take it off the fire, and pour off all the water that remains. Set the pot in the chimney corner with the lid off, while dinner is dishing, that it may have time to dry. You may toss it up lightly with two forks, to separate the grains while it is drying, but do not stir it with a spoon.

A PILAU.

Take a large fine fowl, and cover the breast with slices of fat bacon or ham, secured by skewers. Put it into a stew-pan with two sliced onions. Season it to your taste with white pepper and mace. Have ready a pint of rice that has been well picked, washed, and soaked. Cover the fowl with it. Put in as much water as will well cover the whole. Stew it about half an hour, or till the fowl and rice are thoroughly done; keeping the stew-pan closely covered. Dish it all together, either with the rice covering the fowl, or laid round it in little heaps.

You may make a pilau of beef or mutton with a larger quantity of rice; which must not be put in at first, or it will be done too much, the meat requiring a longer time to stew.

CHICKEN SALAD.

The fowls for this purpose should be young and fine. You may either boil or roast them. They must be quite cold. Having removed all the skin and fat, and disjointed the fowls cut the meat from the bones into very small pieces, not exceeding an inch. Wash and split two large fine heads of celery, and cut the white part into pieces also about an inch long; and having mixed the chicken and celery together, put them into a deep china dish, cover it and set it away.

It is best not to prepare the dressing till just before the salad is to be eaten, that it may be as fresh as possible. Have ready the yolks of eight hard-boiled eggs. Put them into a flat dish, and mash them to a paste with the back of a wooden spoon. Add to the egg a small tea-spoonful of fine salt, the same quantity of cayenne pepper, half a jill of made mustard, a jill or a wine-glass and a half of vinegar, and rather more than two wine-glasses of sweet oil. Mix all these ingredients thoroughly; stirring them a long time till they are quite smooth.

The dressing should not be put on till a few minutes before the salad is sent in; as by lying in it the chicken and celery will become tough and hard. After you pour it on, mix the whole well together with a silver fork.

Chicken salad should be accompanied with plates of bread and butter, and a plate of crackers. It is a supper dish, and is brought in with terrapin, oysters, &c.

Cold turkey is excellent prepared as above.

An inferior salad may be made with cold fillet of veal, instead of chickens.

Cold boiled lobster is very fine cut up and drest in this manner, only substituting for celery, lettuce cut up and mixed with the lobster.

TO ROAST A PAIR OF DUCKS.

After the ducks are drawn, wipe out the inside with a clean cloth, and prepare your stuffing. Mince very fine some green sage leaves, and twice their quantity of onion, (which should first be parboiled,) and add a little butter, and a seasoning of pepper and salt. Mix the whole very well, and fill the crops and bodies of the ducks with it, leaving a little space for the stuffing to swell. Reserve the livers, gizzards, and hearts to put in the gravy. Tie the bodies of the ducks firmly round with strings, (which should be wetted or buttered to keep them from burning,) and put them on the spit before a clear brisk fire. Baste them first with a little salt and water, and then with their own gravy, dredging them lightly with flour at the last. They will be done in about an hour. After boiling the livers, gizzards and hearts, chop them, and put them into the gravy; having first skimmed it, and thickened it with a little browned flour.

Send to table with the ducks a small tureen of onion-sauce with chopped sage leaves in it. Accompany them also with stewed cranberries and green peas.

Canvas-back ducks are roasted in the same manner, omitting the stuffing. They will generally be done enough in three quarters of an hour. Send currant jelly to table with them, and have heaters to place under the plates. Add to the gravy a little cayenne, and a large wine-glass of claret or port.

Other wild ducks and teal may be roasted in about half an hour. Before cooking soak them all night in salt and water, to draw out whatever fishy or sedgy taste they may happen to have, and which may otherwise render them uneatable. Then early in the morning put them in fresh water (without salt,) changing it several times before you spit them.

You may serve up with wild ducks, &c. orange-sauce, which is made by boiling in a little water two large sweet oranges cut into slices, having first removed the rind. When the pulp is all dissolved, strain and press it through a sieve, and add to it the juice of two more oranges, and a little sugar. Send it to table either warm or cold.

STEWED DUCK.

Half roast a large duck. Cut it up, and put it into a stew-pan with a pint of beef-gravy, or dripping of roast-beef. Have ready two boiled onions, half a handful of sage leaves, and two leaves of mint, all chopped very fine and seasoned with pepper and salt. Lay these ingredients over the duck. Stew it slowly for a quarter of an hour. Then put in a quart of young green peas. Cover it closely, and simmer it half an hour longer, till the peas are quite soft. Then add a piece of butter rolled in flour; quicken the fire, and give it one boil. Serve up all together.

A cold duck that has been under-done may be stewed in this manner.

TO HASH A DUCK.

Cut up the duck and season it with pepper and mixed spices. Have ready some thin slices of cold ham or bacon. Place a layer of them in a stew-pan; then put in the duck and cover it with ham. Add just water enough to moisten it, and pour over all a large glass of red wine. Cover the pan closely and let it stew for an hour.

Have ready a quart or more of green peas, boiled tender drained, and mixed with butter and pepper. Lay them round the hashed duck.

If you hash a cold duck in this manner, a quarter of an hour will be sufficient for stewing it; it having been cooked already.

TO ROAST A GOOSE.

Having drawn and singed the goose, wipe out the inside with a cloth, and sprinkle in some pepper and salt. Make a stuffing of four good sized onions minced fine, and half their quantity of green sage leaves minced also, a large tea-cupful of grated bread-crumbs, a piece of butter the size of a walnut, and the beaten yolks of two eggs, with a little pepper and salt. Mix the whole together, and incorporate them well. Put the stuffing into the goose, and press it in hard; but do not entirely fill up the cavity, as the mixture will swell in cooking. Tie the goose securely round with a greased or wetted string; and paper the breast to prevent it from scorching. Fasten the goose on the spit at both ends. The fire must be brisk and well kept up. It will require from two hours to two and a half to roast. Baste it at first with a little salt and water, and then with its own gravy. Take off the paper when the goose is about half done, and dredge it with a little flour towards the last. Having parboiled the liver and heart, chop them and put them into the gravy, which must be skimmed well and thickened with a little browned flour.

Send apple-sauce to table with the goose; also mashed potatoes.

A goose may be stuffed entirely with potatoes, boiled and mashed with milk, butter, pepper and salt.

You may make a gravy of the giblets, that is the neck, pinions, liver, heart and gizzard, stewed in a little water, thickened with butter rolled in flour, and seasoned with pepper and salt. Add a glass of red wine. Before you send it to table, take out all but the liver and heart; mince them and leave them in the gravy. This gravy is by many preferred to that which comes from the goose in roasting. It is well to have both.

If a goose is old it is useless to cook it, as when hard and tough it cannot be eaten.

A GOOSE PIE.

Cut a fine large young goose into eight pieces, and season it with pepper. Reserve the giblets for gravy. Take a smoked tongue that has been all night in soak, parboil it, peel it, and cut it into thick slices, omitting the root, which you must divide into small pieces, and put into a sauce-pan with the giblets and sufficient water to stew them slowly.

Make a nice paste, allowing a pound and a half of butter to three pounds of flour. Roll it out thick, and line with it the bottom and sides of a deep dish. Fill it with the pieces of goose, and the slices of tongue. Skim the gravy you have drawn from the giblets, thicken it with a little browned flour, and pour it into the pie dish. Then put on the lid or upper crust. Notch and ornament it handsomely with leaves and flowers of paste. Bake the pie about three hours in a brisk oven.

In making a large goose pie you may add a fowl, or a pair of pigeons, or partridges,—all cut up.

A duck pie may be made in the same manner.

Small pies are sometimes made of goose giblets only.

A CHRISTMAS GOOSE PIE.

These pies are always made with a standing crust. Put into a sauce-pan one pound of butter cut up, and a pint and a half of water; stir it while it is melting, and let it come to a boil. Then skim off whatever milk or impurity may rise to the top. Have ready four pounds of flour sifted into a pan. Make a hole in the middle of it, and pour in the melted butter while hot. Mix it with a spoon to a stiff paste, (adding the beaten yolks of three or four eggs,) and then knead it very well with your hands, on the paste-board, keeping it dredged with flour till it ceases to be sticky. Then set it away to cool.

Split a large goose, and a fowl down the back, loosen the flesh all over with a sharp knife, and take out all the bones. Parboil a smoked tongue; peel it and cut off the root. Mix together a powdered nutmeg, a quarter of an ounce of powdered mace, a tea-spoonful of pepper, and a tea-spoonful of salt, and season with them the fowl and the goose.

Roll out the paste near an inch thick, and divide it into three pieces. Cut out two of them of an oval form for the top and bottom; and the other into a long straight piece for the sides or walls of the pie. Brush the paste all over with beaten white of egg, and set on the bottom the piece that is to form the wall, pinching the edges together, and cementing them with white of egg. The bottom piece must be large enough to turn up a little round the lower edge of the wall piece, to which it must be firmly joined all round. When you have the crust properly fixed, so as to be baked standing alone without a dish, put in first the goose, then the fowl, and then the tongue. Fill up what space is left with pieces of the flesh of pigeons, or of partridges, quails, or any game that is convenient. There must be no bones in the pie. You may add also some bits of ham, or some force-meat balls. Lastly, cover the other ingredients with half a pound of butter, and pat on the top crust, which, of course, must be also of an oval form to correspond with the bottom. The lid must be placed not quite on the top edge of the wall, but an inch and a half below it. Close it very well, and ornament the sides and top with festoons and leaves cut out of paste. Notch the edges handsomely, and put a paste flower in the centre. Glaze the whole with beaten yolk of egg, and bind the pie all round with a double fold of white paper. Set it in a regular oven, and bake it four hours.

This is one way of making the celebrated goose pies that it is customary in England to send as presents at Christmas. They are eaten at luncheon, and if the weather is cold, and they are kept carefully covered up from the air, they will be good for two or three weeks; the standing crust assisting to preserve them.

TO ROAST A TURKEY.

Make a force-meat of grated bread-crumbs, minced suet, sweet marjoram, grated lemon-peel, nutmeg, pepper, salt, and beaten yolk of egg. You may add some grated cold ham. Light some writing paper, and singe the hairs from the skin of the turkey. Reserve the neck, liver, and gizzard for the gravy. Stuff the craw of the turkey with the force-meat, of which there should be enough made to form into balls for frying, laying them round the turkey when it is dished. Dredge it with flour, and roast it before a clear brisk fire, basting it with cold lard. Towards the last, set the turkey nearer to the fire, dredge it again very lightly with flour, and baste it with butter. It will require, according to its size, from two to three hours roasting.

Make the gravy of the giblets cut in pieces, seasoned, and stewed for two hours in a very little water; thicken it with a spoonful of browned flour, and stir into it the gravy from the dripping-pan, having first skimmed off the fat.

A turkey should be accompanied by ham or tongue. Serve up with it mushroom-sauce. Have stewed cranberries on the table to eat with it. Do not help any one to the legs, or drum-sticks as they are called.

Turkeys are sometimes stuffed entirely with sausage-meat. Small cakes of this meat should then be fried, and laid round it.

To bone a turkey, you must begin with a very sharp knife at the top of the wings, and scrape the flesh loose from the bone without dividing or cutting it to pieces. If done carefully and dexterously, the whole mass of flesh may be separated from the bone, so that you can take hold of the head and draw out the entire skeleton at once. A large quantity of force-meat having been prepared, stuff it hard into the turkey, restoring it by doing so to its natural form, filling out the body, breast, wings and legs, so as to resemble their original shape when the bones were in. Roast or bake it; pouring a glass of port wine into the gravy. A boned turkey is frequently served up cold, covered with lumps of currant jelly; slices of which are laid round the dish.

Any sort of poultry or game may be boned and stuffed in the same manner,

A cold turkey that has not been boned is sometimes sent to table larded all over the breast with slips of fat bacon, drawn through the flesh with a larding needle, and arranged in regular form.

TO BOIL A TURKEY.

Take twenty-five large fine oysters, and chop them. Mix with them half a pint of grated bread-crumbs, half a handful of chopped parsley, a quarter of a pound of butter, two table-spoonfuls, of cream or rich milk, and the beaten yolks of three eggs. When it is thoroughly mixed, stuff the craw of the turkey with it, and sew up the skin. Then dredge it with flour, put it into a large pot or kettle, and cover it well with cold water. Place it over the fire, and let it boil slowly for half an hour, taking off the scum as it rises. Then remove the pot from over the fire, and set it on hot coals to stew slowly for two hours, or two hours and a half, according to its size, Just before you send it to table, place it again over the fire to get well heated. When you boil a turkey, skewer the liver and gizzard to the sides, under the wings.

Send it to table with oyster-sauce in a small tureen.

In making the stuffing, you may substitute for the grated bread, chestnuts boiled, peeled, and minced or mashed. Serve up chestnut-sauce, made by peeling some boiled chestnuts and putting them whole into melted butter,

Some persons, to make them white, boil their turkeys tied up in a large cloth sprinkled with flour.

With a turkey, there should be on the table a ham, or a smoked tongue.

TO ROAST PIGEONS.

Draw and pick four pigeons immediately after they are killed, and let them be cooked soon, as they do not keep well. Wash the inside very clean, and wipe it dry. Stuff them with a mixture of parsley parboiled and chopped, grated bread-crumbs, and butter; seasoned with pepper, salt, and nutmeg. Dredge them with flour, and roast them before a good fire, basting them with butter. They will be done in about twenty-five or thirty minutes. Serve them up with parsley-sauce. Lay the pigeons on the dish in a row.

If asparagus is in season, it will be much better than parsley both for the stuffing and sauce. It must first be boiled. Chop the green heads for the stuffing, and cut them in two for the melted butter. Have cranberry-sauce on the table.

Pigeons may be split and broiled, like chickens; also stewed or fricasseed.

They are very good stewed with slices of cold ham and green peas, serving up all in the same dish.

PIGEON PIE.

Take four pigeons, and pick and clean them very nicely, Season them with pepper and salt, and put inside of every one a large piece of butter and the yolk of a hard-boiled egg. Have ready a good paste, allowing a pound of butter to two pounds of sifted flour. Roll it out rather thick, and line with it the bottom and sides of a large deep dish. Put in the pigeons, and lay on the top some bits of butter rolled in flour. Pour in nearly enough of water to fill the dish. Cover the pie with a lid of paste rolled out thick, and nicely notched, and ornamented with paste leaves and flowers.

You may make a similar pie of pheasants, partridges, or grouse.

TO ROAST PHEASANTS, PARTRIDGES, QUAILS, OR GROUSE.

Pick and draw the birds immediately after they are brought in. Before you roast them, fill the inside with pieces of a fine ripe orange, leaving out the rind and seeds. Or stuff them with grated cold ham, mixed with breadcrumbs, butter, and a little yolk of egg. Lard them with small slips of the fat of bacon drawn through the flesh with a larding needle, Roast them before a clear fire.

Make a fine rich gravy of the trimmings of meat or poultry, stewed in a little water, and thickened with a spoonful of browned flour. Strain it, and set it on the fire again, having added half a pint of claret, and the juice of two large oranges. Simmer it for a few minutes, pour some of it into the dish with the game, and serve the remainder in a boat.

If you stuff them with force-meat, you may, instead of larding, brush them all over with beaten yolk of egg, and then cover them, with breadcrumbs grated finely and sifted.

ANOTHER WAY TO ROAST PHEASANTS, PARTRIDGES, ETC.

Chop some fine raw oysters, omitting the hard part; mix them with salt, and nutmeg, and add some beaten yolk of egg to bind the other ingredients. Cut some very thin slices of cold ham or bacon, and cover the birds with them; then wrap them closely in sheets of white paper well buttered, put them on the spit, and roast them before a clear fire.

Send them to table with oyster-sauce in a boat.

Pies may be made of any of these birds in the same manner as a pigeon pie.

TO ROAST SNIPES, WOODCOCKS, OR PLOVERS.

Pick them immediately; but it is the fashion to cook these birds without drawing. Cut some slices of bread, allowing a slice to each bird, and (having pared off the crust) toast them nicely, and lay them in the bottom of the dripping-pan to catch the trail, as it is called. Dredge the birds with flour, and put them on a small spit before a clear brisk fire. Baste them with lard, or fresh butter. They will be done in twenty or thirty minutes. Serve them up laid on the toast, and garnished with sliced orange, or with orange jelly.

Have brown gravy in a boat.

TO ROAST REED-BIRDS, OR ORTOLANS.

Put into every bird, an oyster, or a little butter mixed with some finely sifted bread-crumbs. Dredge them with flour. Run a small skewer through them, and tie them on the spit. Baste them with lard or with fresh butter. They will be done in about ten minutes.

A very nice way of cooking these birds is, (having greased them all over with lard or with fresh butter, and wrapped them in vine leaves secured closely with a string,) to lay them in a heated iron pan, and bury them in ashes hot enough to roast or bake them. Remove the vine leaves before you send the birds to table.

Reed birds are very fine made into little dumplings with a thin crust of flour and butter, and boiled about twenty minutes. Each must be tied in a separate cloth.

LARDING.

To lard meat or poultry is to introduce into the surface of the flesh, slips of the fat only of bacon, by means of a larding-pin or larding-needle, it being called by both names. It is a steel instrument about a foot long, sharp at one end, and cleft at the other into four divisions, which are near two inches in length, and resemble tweezers. It can be obtained at the hardware stores.

Cut the bacon into slips about two inches in length, half an inch in breadth, and half an inch in thickness. If intended for poultry, the slips of bacon should not be thicker than a straw. Put them, one at a time, into the cleft or split end of the larding-needle. Give each slip a slight twist, and press it down hard into the needle with your fingers. Then push the needle through the flesh, (avoiding the places where the bones are,) and when you draw it out it will have left behind it the slip of bacon sticking in the surface. Take care to have all the slips of the same size, and arranged in regular rows at equal distances. Every slip should stand up about an inch. If any are wrong, take them out and do them over again. To lard handsomely and neatly requires practice and dexterity.

Fowls and game are generally larded on the breast only. If cold, they can be done with the fat of cold boiled ham. Larding may be made to look very tastefully on any thing that is not to be cooked afterwards.

FORCE-MEAT BALLS.

To a pound of the lean of a leg of veal, allow a pound of beef suet. Mince them together very fine. Then season it to your taste with pepper, salt, mace, nutmeg, and chopped sage or sweet marjoram. Then chop a half-pint of oysters, and beat six eggs very well. Mix the whole together, and pound it to a paste in a marble mortar. If you do not want it immediately, put it away in a stone pot, strew a little flour on the top, and cover it closely.

When you wish to use the force-meat, divide into equal parts as much of it as you want; and having floured your hands, roll it into round balls, all of the same size. Either fry them in butter, or boil them.

This force-meat will be found a very good stuffing for meat or poultry.

GRAVY AND SAUCES.

DRAWN OR MADE GRAVY.

For this purpose you may use coarse pieces of the lean of beef or veal, or the giblets and trimmings of poultry or game. If must be stewed for a long time, skimmed, strained, thickened, and flavoured with whatever condiments are supposed most suited to the dish it is to accompany.

In preparing meat to stew for gravy, beat it with a mallet or meat-beetle, score it, and cut it into small pieces; this makes it give oat the juices. Season it with pepper and salt, and put it into a stew-pan with butter only. Heat it gradually, till it becomes brown. Shake the pan frequently, and see that it does not bum or stick to the bottom. It will generally be browned sufficiently in half an hour. Then put in some boiling water, allowing one pint to each pound of meat. Simmer it on coals by the side of the fire for near three hours, skimming it well, and keeping it closely covered. When done, remove it from the heat, let it stand awhile to settle, and then strain it.

If you wish to keep it two or three days, (which you may in winter,) put it into a stone vessel, cover it closely, and set it in a cool place.

Do not thicken this gravy till you go to use it.

MELTED BUTTER, SOMETIMES CALLED DRAWN BUTTER.

Melted butter is the foundation of most of the common sauces. Have a covered sauce-pan for this purpose. One lined with porcelain will be best. Take a quarter of a pound of the best fresh butter, cut it up, and mix with it about two tea-spoonfuls of flour. When it is thoroughly mixed, put it into the sauce-pan, and add to it four table-spoonfuls of cold water. Cover the sauce-pan, and set it in a large tin pan of boiling water. Shake it round continually (always moving it the same way) till it is entirely melted and begins to simmer. Then let it rest till it boils up.

If you set it on hot coals, or over the fire, it will be oily.

If the butter and flour is not well mixed it will be lumpy.

If you put too much water, it will be thin and poor. All these defects are to be carefully avoided.

In melting butter for sweet or pudding sauce, you may use milk instead of water.

TO BROWN FLOUR.

Spread some fine flour on a plate, and set it in the oven, turning it up and stirring it frequently that it may brown equally all through.

Put it into a jar, cover it well, and keep it to stir into gravies to thicken and colour them.

TO BROWN BUTTER.

Put a lump of butter into a frying-pan, and toss it round over the fire till it becomes brown. Then dredge some browned flour over it, and stir it round with a spoon till it boils. It must be made quite smooth. You may make this into a plain sauce for fish by adding cayenne and some flavoured vinegar.

PLAIN SAUCES.

LOBSTER SAUCE.

Boil a dozen blades of mace and half a dozen pepper-corns in about a jill and a half (or three wine-glasses) of water, till all the strength of the spice is extracted. Then strain it, and having cut three quarters of a pound of butter into little bits, melt it in this water, dredging in a little flour as you hold it over the fire to boil. Toss it round, and let it just boil up and no more.

Take a cold boiled lobster,—pound the coral in a mortar adding a little sweet oil. Then stir it into the melted butter.

Chop the meat of the body into very small pieces, and rub it through a cullender into the butter. Cut up the flesh of the claws and tail into dice, and stir it in. Give it another boil up, and it will be ready for table.

Serve it up with fresh salmon, or any boiled fish of the best kind.

Crab sauce is made in a similar manner; also prawn and shrimp sauce.

ANCHOVY SAUCE.

Soak eight anchovies for three or four hours, changing the water every hour. Then put them into a sauce-pan with a quart of cold water. Set them on hot coals and simmer them till they are entirely dissolved, and till the liquid is diminished two-thirds. Then strain it, stir two glasses of red wine, and add to it about half a pint of melted butter.

Heat it over again, and send it to table with salmon or fresh cod.

CELERY SAUCE.

Take a large bunch of young celery. Wash and pare it very clean. Cut it into pieces, and boil it gently in a small quantity of water, till it is quite tender. Then add a little powdered mace and nutmeg, and a very little pepper and salt. Take a tolerably large piece of butter, roll it well in flour, and stir it into the sauce. Boil it up again, and it is ready to send to table.

You may make it with cream, thus:—Prepare and boil your celery as above, adding some mace, nutmeg, a piece of butter the size of a walnut, rolled in flour; and half a pint of cream. Boil all together.

Celery sauce is eaten with boiled poultry.

When celery is out of season, you may use celery seed, boiled in the water which you afterwards use for the melted butter, but strained out after boiling.

NASTURTIAN SAUCE.

This is by many considered superior to caper sauce and is eaten with boiled mutton. It is made with the green seeds of nasturtians, pickled simply in cold vinegar.

Cut about six ounces of butter into small hits, and put them into a small sauce-pan. Mix with a wine-glass of water sufficient flour to make a thick batter, pour it on the butter, and hold the sauce-pan over hot coals, shaking it quickly round, till the butter is melted. Let it just boil up, and then take it from the fire. Thicken it with the pickled nasturtians and send it to table in a boat.

Never pour melted butter over any thing, but always send it to table in a sauce-tureen or boat.

WHITE ONION SAUCE.

Peel a dozen onions, and throw them into salt and water to keep them white. Then boil them tender. When done, squeeze the water from them, and chop them. Have ready some butter that has been melted rich and smooth with milk or cream instead of water. Put the onions into the melted butter, and boil them up at once. If you wish to have them very mild, put in a turnip with them at the first boiling.

Young white onions, if very small, need not be chopped, but may be put whole into the butter.

Use this sauce for rabbits, tripe, boiled poultry, or any boiled fresh meat.

BROWN ONION SAUCE.

Slice some large mild Spanish onions. Cover them with butter, and set them over a slow fire to brown. Then add salt and cayenne pepper to your taste, and some good brown gravy of roast meat, poultry or game, thickened with a bit of butter rolled in flour that has first been browned by holding it in a hot pan or shovel over the fire. Give it a boil, skim it well, and just before you take it off, stir in a half glass of port or claret, and the same quantity of mushroom catchup.

Use this sauce for roasted poultry, game, or meat.

MUSHROOM SAUCE.

Wash a pint of small button mushrooms,—remove the stems and the outside skin. Stew them slowly in veal gravy or in milk or cream, seasoning them with pepper and salt, and adding a piece of butter rolled in a large proportion of flour. Stew them till quite tender, now and then taking off the cover of the pan to stir them.

The flavour will be heightened by having salted a few the night before in a covered dish, to extract the juice, and then stirring it into the sauce while stewing.

This sauce may be served up with poultry, game, or beef-steaks.

In gathering mushrooms take only those that are of a dull pearl colour on the outside, and that have the under part tinged with pale pink.

Boil an onion with them. If there is a poisonous one among them, the onion will turn black. Then throw away the whole.

EGG SAUCE.

Boil four eggs a quarter of an hour. Dip them into cold water to prevent their looking blue. Peel off the shell. Chop the yolks of all, and the whites of two, and stir them into melted butter. Serve this sauce with boiled poultry or fish.

BREAD SAUCE.

Put some grated crumbs of stale bread into a sauce-pan, and pour over them some of the liquor in which poultry or fresh meat has been boiled.

Add some plums or dried currants that have been picked and washed. Having simmered them till the bread is quite soft, and the currants well plumped, add melted butter or cream.

This sauce is for a roast pig.

MINT SAUCE.

Take a large bunch of young green mint; if old the taste will be unpleasant. Wash it very clean. Pick all the leaves from the stalks. Chop the leaves very fine, and mix them with cold vinegar, and a large proportion of powdered sugar. There must be merely sufficient vinegar to moisten the mint well, but by no means enough to make the sauce liquid.

It is only eaten in the spring with roast lamb. Send it to table in a sauce-tureen.

CAPER SAUCE.

Take two large table-spoonfuls of capers and a little vinegar. Stir them for some time into half a pint of thick melted butter.

This sauce is for boiled mutton.

If you happen to have no capers, pickled cucumber chopped fine, or the pickled pods of radish seeds, may be stirred into the butter as a tolerable substitute.

PARSLEY SAUCE.

Wash a bunch of parsley in cold water. Then boil it about six or seven minutes in salt and water. Drain it, cut the leaves from the stalks, and chop them fine. Hare ready some melted butter, and stir in the parsley. Allow two small table-spoonfuls of leaves to half a pint of butter.

Serve it up with boiled fowls, rock-fish, sea-bass, and other boiled fresh fish.. Also with knuckle of veal, and with calf's head boiled plain.

APPLE SAUCE.

Pare, core, and slice some fine apples. Put them into a sauce-pan with just sufficient water to keep them from burning, and some grated lemon-peel. Stew them till quite soft and tender. Then mash them to a paste, and make them very sweet with brown sugar, adding a small piece of butter and some nutmeg.

Apple sauce is eaten with roast pork, roast goose and roast ducks.

Be careful not to have it thin and watery.

CRANBERRY SAUCE.

Wash a quart of ripe cranberries, and put them into a pan with about a wine-glass of water. Stew them slowly, and stir them frequently, particularly after they begin to burst. They require a great deal of stewing, and should be like a marmalade when done. Just before you take them from the fire, stir in a pound of brown sugar.

When they are thoroughly done, put them into a deep dish, and set them away to get cold.

You may strain the pulp through a cullender or sieve into a mould, and when it is in a firm shape send it to table on a glass dish. Taste it when it is cold, and if not sweet enough, add more sugar. Cranberries require more sugar than any other fruit, except plums.

Cranberry sauce is eaten with roast turkey, roast fowls, and roast ducks.

PEACH SAUCE.

Take a quart of dried peaches, (those are richest and best that are dried with the skins on,) and soak them in cold water till they are tender. Then drain them, and put them into a covered pan with a very little water. Set them on coals, and simmer them till they are entirely dissolved. Then mash them with brown sugar, and send them to table cold to eat with roast meat, game or poultry.

WINE SAUCE.

Have ready some rich thick melted or drawn butter, and the moment you take it from the fire, stir in two large glasses of white wine, two tablespoonfuls of powdered white sugar, and a powdered nutmeg. Serve it up with plum pudding, or any sort of boiled pudding that is made of a batter.

COLD SWEET SAUCE.

Stir together, as for a pound-cake, equal quantities of fresh butter and powdered white sugar. When quite light and creamy, add some powdered cinnamon or nutmeg, and a few drops of essence of lemon. Send it to table in a small deep plate with a tea-spoon in it.

Eat it with batter pudding, bread pudding, Indian pudding, &c. whether baked or boiled. Also with boiled apple pudding or dumplings, and with fritters and pancakes.

CREAM SAUCE.

Boil a pint and a half of rich cream with four table-spoonfuls of powdered sugar, some pieces of cinnamon, and a dozen bitter almonds or peach kernels slightly broken up, or a dozen fresh peach leaves. As soon as it has boiled up, take it off the fire and strain it. If it is to be eaten with boiled pudding or with dumplings send it to table hot, but let it get quite cold if you intend it as an accompaniment to fruit pies or tarts.

OYSTER SAUCE.

Take a pint of oysters, and save out a little of their liquid. Put them with their remaining liquor, and some mace and nutmegs, into a covered sauce-pan, and simmer them on hot coals about eight minutes. Then drain them.

Having prepared in another sauce-pan some drawn or melted butter, (mixed with oyster liquor instead of water,) pour it into a sauce-boat, add the oysters to it, and serve it up with boiled poultry or with boiled fresh fish.

STORE FISH SAUCES.

GENERAL REMARKS.

Store fish sauces if properly made will keep for many months. They may be brought to table in fish castors, but a customary mode is to send them round in the small black bottles in which they have been originally deposited. They are in great variety, and may be purchased of the grocers that sell oil, pickles, anchovies, &c. In making them at home, the few following receipts may be found useful.

The usual way of eating these sauces is to pour a little on your plate, and mix it with the melted butter. They give flavour to fish that would otherwise be insipid, and are in general use at genteel tables.

Two table-spoonfuls of any of these sauces may be added to the melted butter a minute before you take it from the fire. But if brought to table in bottles, the company can use it or omit it as they please.

SCOTCH SAUCE.

Take fifteen anchovies, chop them fine, and steep them in vinegar for a week, keeping the vessel closely covered. Then put them into a pint of claret or port wine. Scrape fine a large stick of horseradish, and chop two onions, a handful of parsley, a tea-spoonful of the leaves of lemon-thyme, and two large peach leaves. Add a nutmeg, six or eight blades of mace, nine cloves, and a tea-spoonful of black pepper, all slightly pounded in a mortar. Put all these ingredients into a silver or block tin sauce-pan, or into an earthen pipkin, and add a few grains of cochineal to colour it. Pour in a large half pint of the best vinegar, and simmer it slowly till the bones of the anchovies are entirely dissolved.

Strain the liquor through a sieve, and when quite cold put it away for use in small bottles; the corks dipped in melted rosin, and well-secured by pieces of leather tied closely over them. Fill each bottle quite full, as it will keep the better for leaving no vacancy.

This sauce will give a fine flavour to melted butter.

QUIN'S SAUCE.

Pound in a mortar six large anchovies, moistening them with their own pickle. Then chop and pound six small onions. Mix them with a little black pepper and a little cayenne, half a glass of soy, four glasses of mushroom catchup, two glasses of claret, and two of black walnut pickle. Put the mixture into a small sauce-pan or earthen pipkin, and let it simmer slowly till all the bones of the anchovies are dissolved. Strain it, and when cold, bottle it for use; dipping the cork in melted rosin, and tying leather over it. Fill the bottles quite full.

KITCHINER'S FISH SAUCE.

Mix together a pint of claret, a pint of mushroom catchup, and half a pint of walnut pickle, four ounces of pounded anchovy, an ounce of fresh lemon-peel pared thin, and the same quantity of shalot or small onion. Also an ounce of scraped horseradish, half an ounce of black pepper, and half an ounce of allspice mixed, and the same quantity of cayenne and celery-seed. Infuse these ingredients in a wide-mouthed bottle (closely stopped) for a fortnight, shaking the mixture every day. Then strain and bottle it for use. Put it up in small bottles, filling them quite full.

HARVEY'S SAUCE.

Dissolve six anchovies in a pint of strong vinegar, and then add to them three table-spoonfuls of India soy, and three table-spoonfuls of mushroom catchup, two heads of garlic bruised small, and a quarter of an ounce of cayenne. Add sufficient cochineal powder to colour the mixture red. Let all these ingredients infuse in the vinegar for a fortnight, shaking it every day, and then strain and bottle it for use. Let the bottles be small, and cover the corks with leather.

GENERAL SAUCE.

Chop six shalots or small onions, a clove of garlic, two peach leaves, a few sprigs of lemon-thyme and of sweet basil, and a few bits of fresh orange-peel. Bruise in a mortar a quarter of an ounce of cloves, a quarter of an ounce of mace, and half an ounce of long pepper. Mix two ounces of salt, a jill of vinegar, the juice of two lemons, and a pint of Madeira. Put the whole of these ingredients together in a stone jar, very closely covered. Let it stand all night over embers by the side of the fire. In the morning pour off the liquid quickly and carefully from the lees or settlings, strain it and put it into small bottles, dipping the corks in melted rosin.

This sauce is intended to flavour melted butter or gravy, for every sort of fish and meat.

PINK SAUCE.

Mix together half a pint of port wine, half a pint of strong vinegar, the juice and grated peel of two large lemons, a quarter of an ounce of cayenne, a dozen blades of mace, and a quarter of an ounce of powdered cochineal. Let it infuse a fortnight, stirring it several times a day. Then boil it ten minutes, strain it, and bottle it for use.

Eat it with any sort of fish or game. It will give a fine pink tinge to melted butter.

CATCHUPS.

LOBSTER CATCHUP.

This catchup, warmed in melted butter, is an excellent substitute for fresh lobster sauce at seasons when the fish cannot he procured, as, if properly made, it will keep a year.

Take a fine lobster that weighs about three pounds. Put it into boiling water, and cook it thoroughly. When it is cold break it up, and extract all the flesh from the shell. Pound the red part or coral in a marble mortar, and when it is well bruised, add the white meat by degrees, and pound that also; seasoning it with a tea-spoonful of cayenne, and moistening it gradually with sherry wine. When it is beaten to a smooth paste, mix it well with the remainder of the bottle of sherry. Put it into wide-mouthed bottles, and on the top of each lay a dessert-spoonful of whole pepper. Dip the corks in melted rosin, and secure them well by tying leather over them.

In using this catchup allow four table-spoonfuls to a common-sized sauce-boat of melted butter. Put in the catchup at the last, and hold it over the fire just long enough to be thoroughly heated.

ANCHOVY CATCHUP.

Bone two dozen anchovies, and then chop them. Put to them ten shalots, or very small onions, cut fine, and a handful of scraped horseradish, with a quarter of an ounce of mace. Add a lemon, cut into slices, twelve cloves, and twelve pepper-corns. Then mix together a pint of red wine, a quart of white wine, a pint of water and half a pint of anchovy liquor. Put the other ingredients into the liquid, and boil it slowly till reduced to a quart. Then strain it, and when cold put it into small bottles, securing the corks with leather.

OYSTER CATCHUP.

Take large salt oysters that have just been opened. Wash them in their own liquor, and pound them, in a mortar, omitting the hard parts. To every pint of the pounded oysters, add a half pint of white wine or vinegar, in which you must give them a boil up, removing the scum as it rises. Then to each quart of the boiled oysters allow a tea-spoonful of beaten white pepper, a salt-spoonful of pounded mace, and cayenne and salt to your taste. Let it boil up for a few minutes, and then pass it through a sieve into an earthen pan. When cold, put it into small bottles, filling them quite full, as it will not keep so well if there is a vacancy at the top. Dip the corks in melted rosin, and tie leather over each.

WALNUT CATCHUP.

Take green walnuts that are young enough to be easily pierced through with a large needle. Having pricked them all in several places, throw them into an earthen pan with a large handful of salt, and barely sufficient water to cover them. Break up and mash them with a potato-beetle, or a rolling-pin. Keep them four days in the salt and water, stirring and mashing them every day. The rinds will now be quite soft. Then scald them with boiling-hot salt and water, and raising the pan on the edge, let the walnut liquor flow away from the shells into another pan. Put the shells into a mortar, and pound them with vinegar, which will extract from them all the remaining juice.

Put all the walnut liquor together, and boil and skim it, then to every quart allow an ounce of bruised ginger, an ounce of black pepper, half an ounce of cloves, and half an ounce of nutmeg, all slightly beaten. Boil the spice and walnut liquor in a closely covered vessel for three quarters of an hour. When cold, bottle it for use, putting equal proportions of the spice into each bottle. Secure the corks with leather.

MUSHROOM CATCHUP.

Take mushrooms that have been freshly gathered, and examine them carefully to ascertain that they are of the right sort. Pick them nicely, and wipe them clean, but do not wash them. Spread a layer of them at the bottom of a deep earthen pan, and then sprinkle them well with salt; then another layer of mushrooms, and another layer of salt, and so on alternately. Throw a folded cloth over the jar, and set it by the fire or in a very cool oven. Let it remain thus for twenty-four hours, and then mash them well with your hands. Next squeeze and strain them through a bag.

To every quart of strained liquor add an ounce and a half of whole black pepper, and boil it slowly in a covered vessel for half an hour. Then add a quarter of an ounce of allspice, half an ounce of sliced ginger, a few cloves, and three or four blades of mace. Boil it with the spice fifteen minutes longer. When it is done, take it off, and let it stand awhile to settle. Pour it carefully off from the sediment and put it into small bottles, filling them to the top. Secure them well with corks dipped in melted rosin, and leather caps tied over them.

The longer catchup is boiled, the better it will keep. You may add cayenne and nutmeg to the spices.

The bottles should be quite small, as it soon spoils after being opened.

TOMATA CATCHUP.

Gather the tomatas on a dry day, and when quite ripe. Peel them, and cut them into quarters. Put them into a large earthen pan, and mash and squeeze them till they are reduced to a pulp. Allowing half a pint of fine salt to a hundred tomatas, put them into a preserving kettle, and boil them gently with the salt for two hours, stirring them frequently to prevent their burning. Then strain them through a fine sieve, pressing them with the back of a silver spoon. Season them to your taste with mace, cinnamon, nutmeg, ginger, and white or red pepper, all powdered fine.

Put the tomata again over the fire with the spices, and boil it slowly till very thick, stirring it frequently.

When cold, put it up in small bottles, secure the corks well, and it will keep good a year or two.

LEMON CATCHUP.

Cut nine large lemons into thin slices, and take out the seeds. Prepare, by pounding them in a mortar, two ounces of mustard seed, half an ounce of black pepper, half an ounce of nutmeg, a quarter of an ounce of mace, and a quarter of an ounce of cloves. Slice thin two ounces of horseradish. Put all these ingredients together. Strew over them three ounces of fine salt. Add a quart of the best vinegar.

Boil the whole twenty minutes. Then put it warm into a jar, and let it stand three weeks closely covered. Stir it up daily.

Then strain it through a sieve, and put it up in small bottles to flavour fish and other sauces. This is sometimes called lemon pickle.

FLAVOURED VINEGARS.

These vinegars will be found very useful, at times when the articles with which they are flavoured cannot be conveniently procured. Care should be taken to have the bottles that contain them accurately labelled, very tightly corked, and kept in a dry place. The vinegar used for these purposes should be of the very best sort.

TARRAGON VINEGAR.

Tarragon should be gathered on a dry day, just before the plant flowers. Pick the green leaves from the stalks, and dry them a little before the fire. Then put them into a wide-mouthed stone jar, and cover them with the best vinegar, filling up the jar. Let it steep fourteen days, and then strain it through a flannel bag. Pour it through a funnel into half-pint bottles, and cork them well.

SWEET BASIL VINEGAR.

Is made precisely in the same manner; also those of green mint, and sweet marjoram.

CELERY VINEGAR.

Pound two ounces of celery seed in a mortar, and steep it for a fortnight in a quart of vinegar. Then strain and bottle it.

BURNET VINEGAR.

Nearly fill a wide-mouthed bottle with the fresh green leaves of burnet, cover them with vinegar, and let them steep two weeks. Then strain off the vinegar, wash the bottle, put in a fresh supply of burnet leaves, pour the same vinegar over them, and let it infuse a fortnight longer. Then strain it again and it will be fit for use. The flavour will exactly resemble that of cucumbers.

HORSERADISH VINEGAR.

Make a quart of the best vinegar boiling hot, and pour it on four ounces of scraped horseradish. Let it stand a week, then strain it off, renew the horseradish, adding the same vinegar cold, and let it infuse a week longer, straining it again at the last.

SHALOT VINEGAR.

Peel and chop fine four ounces of shalots, or small button onions. Pour on them a quart of the best vinegar, and let them steep a fortnight; then strain and bottle it.

Make garlic vinegar in the same manner; using but two ounces of garlic to a quart of vinegar. Two or three drops will be sufficient to impart a garlic taste to a pint of gravy or sauce. More will be offensive. The cook should be cautioned to use it very sparingly, as to many persons it is extremely disagreeable.

CHILLI VINEGAR.

Take a hundred red chillies or capsicums, fresh gathered; cut them into small pieces and infuse them for a fortnight in a quart of the best vinegar, shaking the bottle every day. Then strain it.

RASPBERRY VINEGAR.

Put two quarts of ripe fresh-gathered raspberries into a stone or china vessel, and pour on them a quart of vinegar. Let it stand twenty-four hours, and then strain it through a sieve. Pour the liquid over two quarts of fresh raspberries, and let it again infuse for a day and a night. Then strain it a second time. Allow a pound of loaf sugar to every pint of juice. Break up the sugar, and let it melt in the liquor. Then put the whole into a stone jar, cover it closely, and set it in a kettle of boiling water, which must be kept on a quick boil for an hour. Take off all the scum and when cold, bottle the vinegar for use.

MUSTARD AND PEPPER.

COMMON MUSTARD

Is best when fresh made. Take good flour of mustard; put it in a plate, add to it a little salt, and mix it by degrees with boiling water to the usual consistence, rubbing it for a long time with a broad-bladed knife or a wooden spoon. It should be perfectly smooth. The less that is made at a time the better it will be. If you wish it very mild, use sugar instead of salt, and boiling milk instead of water.

KEEPING MUSTARD.

Dissolve three ounces of salt in a quart of boiling vinegar, and pour it hot upon two ounces of scraped horseradish. Cover the jar closely and let it stand twenty-four hours. Strain it and then mix it by degrees with the best flour of mustard. Make it of the usual thickness, and beat it till quite smooth. Then put it into wide-mouthed bottles and stop it closely.

FRENCH MUSTARD.

Mix together four ounces of the very best mustard powder, four salt-spoons of salt, a large table-spoonful of minced tarragon leaves, and two cloves of garlic chopped fine. Pour on by degrees sufficient vinegar (tarragon vinegar is best) to dilute it to the proper consistence. It will probably require about four wine-glassfuls or half a pint. Mix it well, using for the purpose a wooden spoon. When done, put it into a wide-mouthed bottle or into little white jars. Cork it very closely, and keep it in a dry place. It will not be fit for use in less than two days.

This (used as the common mustard) is a very agreeable condiment for beef or mutton.

VEGETABLES

GENERAL REMARKS.

All vegetables should be well picked and washed. A very little salt should always be thrown into the water in which they are boiled. A steady regular fire should be kept up, and they should never for a moment be allowed to stop boiling or simmering till they are thoroughly done. Every sort of vegetable should be cooked till tender, as if the least hard or under-done they are both unpalatable and unwholesome. The practice of putting pearl-ash in the pot to improve the colour of green vegetables should be strictly forbidden, as it destroys the flavour, and either renders them flat and insipid, or communicates a very disagreeable taste of its own.

Every sort of culinary vegetable is infinitely best when fresh from the garden, and gathered as short a time as possible before it is cooked. They should all be laid in a pan of cold water for a while previous to boiling.

When done, they should be carefully drained before they go to table, or they will be washy all through, and leave puddles of discoloured water in the bottoms of the dishes, to the disgust of the company and the discredit of the cook.

TO BOIL POTATOES.

Potatoes that are boiled together, should be as nearly as possible of the same size. Wash, but do not pare them. Put them into a pot with water enough to cover them about an inch, and do not put on the pot lid. When the water is very near boiling, pour it off, and replace it with the same quantity of cold water, into which throw a good portion of salt. The cold water sends the heat from the surface to the heart, and makes the potatoes mealy. Potatoes of a moderate size will require about half an hour boiling; large ones an hour. Try them with a fork. When done, pour off the water, cover the pot with a folded napkin, or flannel, and let them stand by the fire about a quarter of an hour to dry.

Peel them and send them to table.

Potatoes should not be served up with the skins on. It has a coarse, slovenly look, and disfigures the appearance of the dinner; besides the trouble and inconvenience of peeling them at table.

When the skins crack in boiling, it is no proof that they are done, as too much fire under the pot will cause the skins of some potatoes to break while the inside is hard.

After March, when potatoes are old, it is best to pare them before boiling and to cut out all the blemishes. It is then better to mash them always before they are sent to table. Mash them when quite hot, using a potato-beetle for the purpose; add to them a piece of fresh butter, and a little salt, and, if convenient, some milk, which will greatly improve them. You may score and brown them on the top.

A very nice way of serving up potatoes is, after they are peeled, to pour over them some hot cream in which a very little butter has been melted, and sprinkle them with pepper. This is frequently done in country houses where cream is plenty. New potatoes (as they are called when quite young) require no peeling, but should be well washed and brushed before they are boiled.

FRIED POTATOES.

Take cold potatoes that have been boiled, grate them, make them into flat cakes, and fry them in butter. They are nice at breakfast. You may mix some beaten yolk of egg with them.

Cold potatoes may be fried in slices or quarters, or broiled on a gridiron.

Raw potatoes, when fried, are generally hard, tough, and strong.

POTATO SNOW.

For this purpose use potatoes that are very white, mealy, and smooth. Boil them very carefully, and when they are done, peel them, pour off the water, and set them on a trivet before the fire till they are quite dry and powdery. Then rub them through a coarse wire sieve into the dish on which they are to go to table. Do not disturb the heap of potatoes before it is served up, or the flakes will fall and it will flatten. This preparation looks well; but many think that it renders the potato insipid.

ROASTED POTATOES.

Take large fine potatoes; wash and dry them, and either lay them on the hearth and keep them buried in hot wood ashes, or bake them slowly in a Dutch oven. They will not be done in less than two hours. It will save time to half-boil them before they are roasted. Send them to table with the skins on, and eat them with cold butter and salt. They are introduced with cold meat at supper.

Potatoes keep best buried in sand or earth. They should never be wetted till they are washed for cooking. If you have them in the cellar, see that they are well covered with matting or old carpet, as the frost injures them greatly.

SWEET POTATOES BOILED.

If among your sweet potatoes there should he any that are very large and thick, split them, and cut them in four, that they may not require longer time to cook than the others. Boil them with the skins on in plenty of water, but without any salt. You may set the pot on coals in the corner. Try them with a fork, and see that they are done all through; they will take at least an hour. Then drain off the water, and set them for a few minutes in a tin pan before the fire, or in the stove, that they may be well dried. Peel them before they are sent to table.

FRIED SWEET POTATOES.

Choose them of the largest size. Half boil them, and then having taken off the skins, cut the potatoes in slices, and fry them in butter, or in nice dripping.

Sweet potatoes are very good stewed with fresh pork, veal, or beef.

The best way to keep them through the cold weather, is to bury them in earth or sand; otherwise they will be scarcely eatable after October.

CABBAGE.

All vegetables of the cabbage kind should be carefully washed, and examined in case of insects lurking among the leaves. To prepare a cabbage for boiling, remove the outer leaves, and pare and trim the stalk, cutting it close and short. If the cabbage is large, quarter it; if small, cut it in half; and let it stand for a while in a deep part of cold water with the large end downwards. Put it into a pot with plenty of water, (having first tied it together to keep it whole while boiling,) and, taking off the scum, boil it two hours, or till the stalk is quite tender. When done, drain and squeeze it well. Before you send it to table introduce a little fresh butter between the leaves; or have melted butter in a boat. If it has been boiled with meat add no butter to it.

A young cabbage will boil in an hour or an hour and a half.

CALE-CANNON.

Boil separately some potatoes and cabbage. When done, drain and squeeze the cabbage, and chop or mince it very small. Mash the potatoes, and mix them gradually but thoroughly with the chopped cabbage, adding butter, pepper and salt. There should be twice as much potato as cabbage.

Cale-cannon is eaten with corned beef, boiled pork, or bacon.

Cabbages may be kept good all winter by burying them in a hole dug in the ground.

CAULIFLOWER

Remove the green leaves that surround the head or white part, and peel off the outside skin of the small piece of stalk that is left on. Cut the cauliflower in four, and lay it for an hour in a pan of cold water. Then tie it together before it goes into the pot. Put it into boiling water and simmer it till the stalk is thoroughly tender, keeping it well covered with water, and carefully removing the scum. It will take about two hours.

Take it up as soon as it is done; remaining in the water will discolour it. Drain it well, and send it to table with melted butter.

It will be much whiter if put on in boiling milk and water.

BROCOLI.

Prepare brocoli for boiling in the same manner as cauliflower, leaving the stalks rather longer, and splitting the head in half only. Tie it together again, before it goes into the pot. Put it on in hot water, and let it simmer till the stalk is perfectly tender.

As soon as it is done take it out of the water and drain it. Send melted butter to table with it.

SPINACH.

Spinach requires close examination and picking, as insects are frequently found among it, and it is often gritty. Wash it through three or four waters. Then drain it, and put it on in boiling water. Ten minutes is generally sufficient time to boil spinach. Be careful to remove the scum. When it is quite tender, take it up, and drain and squeeze it well. Chop it fine, and put it into a sauce-pan with a piece of butter and a little pepper and salt. Set it on hot coals, and let it stew five minutes, stirring it all the time.

SPINACH AND EGGS.

Boil the spinach as above, and drain and press it, but do not chop it. Have ready some eggs poached as follows. Boil in a sauce-pan, and skim some clear spring water, adding to it a table-spoonful of vinegar. Break the eggs separately, and having taken the sauce-pan off the fire, slip the eggs one at a time into it with as much dexterity as you can. Let the sauce-pan stand by the side of the fire till the white is set, and then put it over the fire for two minutes. The yolk should be thinly covered by the white. Take them up with an egg slice, and having trimmed the edges of the whites, lay the eggs on the top of the spinach, which should firstly seasoned with pepper and salt and a little butter, and must be sent to table hot.

TURNIPS.

Take off a thick paring from the outside, and boil the turnips gently for an hour and a half. Try them with a fork, and when quite tender, take them up, drain them on a sieve, and either send them to table whole with melted butter, or mash them in a cullender, (pressing and squeezing them well;) season with a little pepper and salt, and mix with them a very small quantity of butter. Setting in the sun after they are cooked, or on a part of the table upon which the sun may happen to shine, will give to turnips a singularly unpleasant taste, and should therefore be avoided.

When turnips are very young, it is customary to serve them up with about two inches of the green top left on them.

If stewed with meat, they should be sliced or quartered.

Mutton, either boiled or roasted, should always be accompanied by turnips.

CARROTS.

Wash and scrape them well. If large cut them into two three, or four pieces. Put them into boiling water with a little salt in it. Full grown carrots will require three hours' boiling; smaller ones two hours, and young ones an hour. Try them with a fork, and when they are tender throughout, take them up and dry them in a cloth. Divide them in pieces and split them, or cut them into slices.

Eat them with melted butter. They should accompany boiled beef or mutton.

PARSNIPS.

Wash, scrape and split them. Put them into a pot of boiling water; add a little salt, and boil them till quite tender, which will be in from two to three hours, according to their size. Dry them in a cloth when done, and pour melted butter over them in the dish. Serve them up with any sort of boiled meat, or with salt cod.

Parsnips are very good baked or stewed with meat.

RUSSIAN OR SWEDISH TURNIPS

This turnip (the Ruta Baga) is very large and of a reddish yellow colour; they are generally much liked. Take off a thick paring, cut the turnips into large pieces, or thick slices, and lay them awhile in cold water. Then boil them gently about two hours, or till they are quite soft. When done, drain, squeeze and mash them, and season them with pepper and salt, and a very little butter. Take care not to set them in a part of the table where the sun comes, as it will spoil the taste.

Russian turnips should always be mashed.

SQUASHES OR CYMLINGS.

The green or summer squash is best when the outside is beginning to turn yellow, as it is then less watery and insipid than when younger. Wash them, cut them into pieces, and take out the seeds. Boil them about three quarters of an hour, or till quits tender. When done, drain and squeeze them well till you have pressed out all the water; mash them with a little butter, pepper and salt. Then put the squash thus prepared into a stew-pan, set it on hot coals, and stir it very frequently till it becomes dry. Take care not to let it burn.

WINTER SQUASH, OR CASHAW.

This is much finer than the summer squash. It is fit to eat in August, and, in a dry warm place, can be kept well all winter. The colour is a very bright yellow. Pare it, take out the seeds, cut it in pieces, and stew it slowly till quite soft, in a very little water. Afterwards drain, squeeze, and press it well, and mash it with a very little butter, pepper and salt.

PUMPKIN.

Deep coloured pumpkins are generally the best. In a dry warm place they can be kept perfectly good all winter. When you prepare to stew a pumpkin, cut it in half and take out all the seeds. Then cut it in thick slices, and pare them. Put it into a pot with a very little water, and stew it gently for an hour, or till soft enough to mash. Then take it out, drain, and squeeze it till it is as dry as you can get it.

Afterwards mash it, adding a little pepper and salt, and a very little butter.

Pumpkin is frequently stewed with fresh beef or fresh pork.

The water in which pumpkin has been boiled, is said to be very good to mix bread with, it having a tendency to improve it in sweetness and to keep it moist.

HOMINY.

Wash the hominy very clean through three or four waters. Then put it into a pot (allowing two quarts of water to one quart of hominy) and boil it slowly five hours. When done, take it up, and drain the liquid from it through a cullender. Put the hominy into a deep dish, and stir into it a small piece of fresh butter.

The small grained hominy is boiled in rather less water, and generally eaten with butter and sugar.

INDIAN CORN.

Corn for boiling should be full grown but young and tender. When the grains become yellow it is too old. Strip it of the outside leaves and the silk, but let the inner leaves remain, as they will keep in the sweetness. Put it into a large pot with plenty of water, and boil it rather fast for three hours or more. When done, drain off the water, and remove the leaves.

You may either lay the ears on a large flat dish and send them to table whole, or broken in half; or you may cut all the corn off the cob, and serve it up in a deep dish, mixed with butter, pepper and salt.

MOCK OYSTERS OF CORN.

Take a dozen and a half ears of large young corn, and grate all the grains off the cob as fine as possible. Mix with the grated corn three large tablespoonfuls of sifted flour, the yolks of six eggs well beaten. Let all be well incorporated by hard beating.

Have ready in a frying-pan an equal proportion of lard and fresh butter. Hold it over the fire till it is boiling hot, and then put in portions of the mixture as nearly as possible in shape and size like fried oysters. Fry them brown, and send them to table hot. They should be near an inch thick.

This is an excellent relish at breakfast, and may be introduced as a side dish at dinner. In taste it has a singular resemblance to fried oysters. The corn must be young.

STEWED EGG PLANT.

The purple egg plants are better than the white ones. Put them whole into a pot with plenty of water, and simmer them till quite tender. Then take them out, drain them, and (having peeled off the skins) cut them up, and mash them smooth in a deep dish. Mix with them some grated bread, some powdered sweet marjoram, and a large piece of butter, adding a few pounded cloves. Grate a layer of bread over the top, and put the dish into the oven and brown it. You must send it to table in the same dish.

Eggplant is sometimes eaten at dinner, but generally at breakfast.

TO FRY EGG PLANT.

Do not pare your egg plants if they are to be fried, but slice them about half an inch thick, and lay them an hour or two in salt and water to remove their strong taste, which to most persons is very unpleasant. Then take them out, wipe them, and season them, with pepper only. Beat some yolk of egg; and in another dish grate a sufficiency of bread-crumbs. Have ready in a frying-pan some lard and batter mixed, and make it boil. Then dip each slice of egg plant first in the egg, and then in the crumbs, till both sides are well covered; and fry them brown, taking care to have them done all through, as the least rawness renders them very unpalatable.

STUFFED EGG PLANTS.

Parboil them to take off their bitterness. Then slit each one down the side, and extract the seeds. Have ready a stuffing made of grated bread-crumbs, butter, minced sweet herbs, salt, pepper, nutmeg, and beaten yolk of egg. Fill with it the cavity from whence you took the seeds, and bake the egg plants in a Dutch oven. Serve them up with a made gravy poured into the dish.

FRIED CUCUMBERS.

Having pared your cucumbers, cut them lengthways into pieces about as thick as a dollar. Then dry them in a cloth. Season them with pepper and salt, and sprinkle them thick with flour. Melt some butter in a frying-pan, and when it boils, put in the slices of cucumber, and fry them of a light brown. Send them to table hot.

They make a breakfast dish..

TO DRESS CUCUMBERS RAW.

They should be as fresh from the vine as possible, few vegetables being more unwholesome when long gathered. As soon as they are brought in lay them in cold water. Just before they are to go to table take them out, pare them and slice them into a pan of fresh cold water. When they are all sliced, transfer them to a deep dish, season them with a little salt and black pepper, and pour over them some of the best vinegar, to which you may add a little salad oil. You may mix with them a small quantity of sliced onion; not to be eaten, but to communicate a slight flavour of onion to the vinegar.

SALSIFY.

Having scraped the salsify roots, and washed them in cold water, parboil them. Then take them out, drain them, cut them into large pieces and fry them in butter.

Salsify is frequently stewed slowly till quite tender, and then served up with melted butter. Or it may be first boiled, then grated, and made into cakes to be fried in butter.

Salsify must not be left exposed to the air, or it will turn blackish.

ARTICHOKES.

Strip off the coarse outer leaves, and cut off the stalks close to the bottom. Wash the artichokes well, and let them lie two or three hours in cold water. Put them with their heads downward into a pot of boiling water, keeping them down by a plate floated over them. They must boil steadily from two to three hours; take care to replenish the pot with additional boiling water as it is wanted. When they are tender all through, drain them, and serve them up with melted butter.

BEETS.

Wash the beets, but do not scrape or cut them while they are raw; for if a knife enters them before they are boiled they will lose their colour. Boil them from two to three hours, according to their size. When they are tender all through, take them up, and scrape off all the outside. If they are young beets they are best split down and cut into long pieces, seasoned with pepper, and sent to table with melted butter. Otherwise you may slice them thin, after they are quite cold, and pour vinegar over them.

TO STEW BEETS.

Boil them first, and then scrape and slice them. Put them into a stew-pan with a piece of butter rolled in flour, some boiled onion and parsley chopped fine, and a little vinegar, salt and pepper. Set the pan on hot coals, and let the beets stew for a quarter of an hour.

TO BOIL GREEN OR FRENCH BEANS.

These beans should be young, tender, and fresh gathered. Remove the strings with a knife, and take off both ends of the bean. Then cut them in two or three pieces only; for if split or cut very small, they become watery and lose much of their taste. They look best when cut slanting. As you cut them, throw them into a pan of cold water, and let them lay awhile. Boil them an hour and a half. They must be perfectly tender before you take them up. Then drain and press them well, season them with pepper, and mix into them a piece of butter.

SCARLET BEANS.

It is not generally known that the pod of the scarlet bean, if green and young, is extremely nice when cut into three or four pieces and boiled. They will require near two hours, and must be drained well, and mixed as before mentioned with butter and pepper. If gathered at the proper time, when the seed is just perceptible, they are superior to any of the common beans.

LIMA BEANS.

These are generally considered the finest of all beans, and should be gathered young. Shell them, lay them in a pan of cold water, and then boil them about two hours, or till they are quite soft. Drain them well, and add to them some butter and a little pepper.

They are destroyed by the first frost, but can be kept during the winter, by gathering them on a dry day when full grown but not the least hard, and putting them in their pods into a keg. Throw some salt into the bottom of the keg, and cover it with a layer of the bean-pods; then add more salt, and then another layer of beans, till the keg is full. Press them down with a heavy weight, cover the keg closely, and keep it in a cool dry place. Before you use them, soak the pods all night in cold water; the next day shell them, and soak the beans till you are ready to boil them.

DRIED BEANS.

Wash them and lay them in soak over night. Early in the morning put them into a pot with plenty of water, and boil them slowly till dinner time. They will require seven or eight hours to be sufficiently done. Then take them off, put them into a sieve, and strain off the liquid.

Send the beans to table in a deep dish, seasoned with pepper, and having a piece of butter mixed with them.

GREEN PEAS.

Green peas are unfit for eating after they become hard and yellowish; but they are better when nearly full grown than when very small and young. They should be gathered as short a time as possible before they are cooked, and laid in cold water as soon as they are shelled. They will require about an hour to boil soft. When quite done, drain them, mix with them a piece of butter, and add a little pepper.

Peas may be greatly improved by boiling with them two or three lumps of loaf-sugar, and a sprig of mint to be taken out before they are dished. This is an English way of cooking green peas, and is to most tastes a very good one.

TO BOIL ONIONS.

Take off the tops and tails, and the thin outer skin; but no more lest the onions should go to pieces. Lay them on the bottom of a pan which is broad enough to contain them without piling one on another; just cover them with water, and let them simmer slowly till they are tender all through, but not till they break.

Serve them up with melted butter.

TO ROAST ONIONS.

Onions are best when parboiled before roasting. Take large onions, place them on a hot hearth and roast them before the fire in their skins, turning them as they require it. Then peel them, send them to table whole, and eat them with butter and salt.

TO FRY ONIONS.

Peel, slice them, and fry them brown in butter or nice dripping.

Onions should be kept in a very dry place, as dampness injures them.

TO BOIL ASPARAGUS.

Large or full grown asparagus is the best. Before you begin to prepare it for cooking, set on the fire a pot with plenty of water, and sprinkle into it a handful of salt. Your asparagus should be all of the same size. Scrape the stalks till they are perfectly nice and white; cut them all of equal length, and short, so as to leave them but two or three inches below the green part. To serve up asparagus with long stalks is now becoming obsolete. As you scrape them, throw them into a pan of cold water. Then tie them up in small bundles with bass or tape, as twine will cut them to pieces. When the water is boiling fast, put in the asparagus, and boil it an hour; if old it will require an hour and a quarter. When it is nearly done boiling, toast a large slice of bread sufficient to cover the dish (first cutting off the crust) and dip it into the asparagus water in the pot. Lay it in a dish, and, having drained the asparagus, place it on the toast with all the heads pointed inwards towards the centre, and the stalks spreading outwards. Serve up melted butter with it.

SEA KALE.

Sea kale is prepared, boiled, and served up in the same manner as asparagus.

POKE.

The young stalks and leaves of the poke-berry plant when quite small and first beginning to sprout up from the ground in the spring, are by most persons considered very nice, and are frequently brought to market. If the least too old they acquire a strong taste, and should not be eaten, as they then become unwholesome. They are in a proper state when the part of the stalk nearest to the ground is not thicker than small asparagus. Scrape the stalks, (letting the leaves remain on them,) and throw them into cold water. Then tie up the poke in bundles, put it into a pot that has plenty of boiling water, and let it boil fast an hour at least. Serve it up with or without toast, and send melted butter with, it in a boat.

STEWED TOMATAS.

Peel your tomatas, cut them in half and squeeze out the seeds. Then put them into a stew-pan without any water, and add to them cayenne and salt to your taste, (and if you choose,) a little minced onion, and some powdered mace, Stew them slowly till they are first dissolved and then dry.

BAKED TOMATAS

Peel some large fine tomatas, cut them up, and take out the seeds. Then put them into a deep dish in alternate layers with grated bread-crumbs, and a very little butter in small bits. There must be a large proportion of bread-crumbs. Season the whole with a little salt, and cayenne pepper. Set it in an oven, and bake it. In cooking tomatas, take care not to have them too liquid.

MUSHROOMS.

Good mushrooms are only found in clear open fields where the air is pure and unconfined. Those that grow in low damp ground, or in shady places, are always poisonous. Mushrooms of the proper sort generally appear in August and September, after a heavy dew or a misty night. They may be known by their being of a pale pink or salmon colour on the gills or under side, while the top is of a dull pearl-coloured white; and by their growing only in open places. When they are a day old, or a few hours after they are gathered, the reddish colour changes to brown.

The poisonous or false mushrooms are of various colours, sometimes of a bright yellow or scarlet all over; sometimes entirely of a chalky white stalk, top, and gills.

It is easy to detect a bad mushroom if all are quite fresh; but after being gathered a few hours the colours change, so that unpractised persons frequently mistake them.

It is said that if you boil an onion among mushrooms the onion will turn of a bluish black when there is a bad one among them. Of course, the whole should then be thrown into the fire. If in stirring mushrooms, the colour of the silver spoon is changed, it is also most prudent to destroy them all.

TO STEW MUSHROOMS.

For this purpose the small button mushrooms are best. Wash them clean, peel off the skin, and cut off the stalks. Put the trimmings into a small sauce-pan with just enough water to keep them from burning, and, covering them closely, let them stew a quarter of an hour. Then strain the liquor, and having put the mushrooms into a clean sauce-pan, (a silver one, or one lined with porcelain,) add the liquid to them with a little nutmeg, pepper and salt, and a piece of butter rolled in flour. Stew them fifteen minutes, and just before you take them up, stir in a very little cream or rich milk and some beaten yolk of egg. Serve them hot. While they are cooking, keep the pan as closely covered as possible.

If you wish to have the full taste of the mushroom only, after washing, trimming, and peeling them, put them into a stew-pan with a little salt and no water. Set them on coals, and stew them slowly till tender, adding nothing to them but a little butter rolled in flour, or else a little cream. Be sure to keep the pan well covered.

BROILED MUSHROOMS.

For this purpose take large mushrooms, and be careful to have them freshly gathered. Peel them, score the under side, and cut off the stems. Lay them one by one in an earthen pan, brushing them over with sweet oil or oiled butter, and sprinkling each with a little pepper and salt. Cover them closely, and let them set for about an hour and a half. Then place them on a gridiron over clear hot coals, and broil them on both sides.

Make a gravy for them of their trimmings stewed in a very little water, strained and thickened with a beaten egg stirred in just before it goes to table.

BOILED RICE.

Pick your rice clean, and wash it in two cold waters, not draining off the last water till you are ready to put the rice on the fire. Prepare a sauce-pan of water with a little salt in it, and when it boils, sprinkle in the rice. Boil it hard twenty minutes, keeping it covered. Then take it from the fire, and pour off the water. Afterwards set the sauce-pan in the chimney-corner with the lid off, while you are dishing your dinner, to allow the rice to dry, and the grains to separate.

Rice, if properly boiled, should be soft and white, and every grain ought to stand alone. If badly managed, it will, when brought to table, be a grayish watery mass.

In most southern families, rice, is boiled every day for the dinner table, and eaten with the meat and poultry.

The above is a Carolina receipt.

TO DRESS LETTUCE AS SALAD.

Strip off the outer leaves, wash the lettuce, split it in half, and lay it in cold water till dinner time. Then drain it and put it into a salad dish. Have ready two eggs boiled hard, (which they will be in twelve minutes,) and laid in a basin of cold water for five minutes to prevent the whites from turning blue. Cut them in half, and lay them on the lettuce.

Put the yolks of the eggs on a large plate, and with a wooden spoon mash them smooth, mixing with them a table-spoonful of water, and two table-spoonfuls of sweet oil. Then add, by degrees, a salt-spoonful of salt, a tea-spoonful of mustard, and a tea-spoonful of powdered loaf-sugar. When these are all smoothly united, add very gradually three table-spoonfuls of vinegar. The lettuce having been cut up fine on another plate, put it to the dressing, and mix it well.

If you have the dressing for salad made before a dinner, put it into the bottom of the salad dish; then (having cut it up) lay the salad upon it, and let it rest till it is to be eaten, as stirring it will injure it.

You may decorate the top of the salad with slices of red beet, and with the hard white of the eggs cut into rings.

CELERY.

Scrape and wash it well, and let it lie in cold water till shortly before it goes to table; then dry it in a cloth, trim it, and split down the stalks almost to the bottom, leaving on a few green leaves. Send it to table in a celery glass, and eat it with salt only; or chop it fine, and make a salad dressing for it.

RADISHES.

To prepare radishes for eating, wash them and lay them in clean cold water as soon as they are brought in. Shortly before they go to table, scrape off the thin outside skin, trim the sharp end, cut off the leaves at the top, leaving the stalks about an inch long, and put them on a small dish. Eat them with salt.

Radishes should not be eaten the day after they are pulled, as they are extremely unwholesome if not quite fresh.

The thick white radishes, after being scraped and trimmed, should be split or cleft in four, half way down from the top.

TO ROAST CHESTNUTS.

The large Spanish chestnuts are the best for roasting. Cut a slit in the shell of every one to prevent their bursting when hot. Put them into a pan, and set them over a charcoal furnace till they are thoroughly roasted; stirring them up frequently and taking care hot to let them burn. When they are done, peel off the shells, and send the chestnuts to table wrapped up in a napkin to keep them warm.

Chestnuts should always be roasted or boiled before they are eaten.

GROUND-NUTS.

These nuts are never eaten raw. Put them, with their shells on, into an iron pan, and set them in an oven; or you may do them in a skillet on hot coals. A large quantity may be roasted in an iron pot over the fire. Stir them frequently, taking one out from time to time, and breaking it to try if they are done.

EGGS, ETC.

TO KEEP EGGS.

There is no infallible mode of ascertaining the freshness of an egg before you break it, but unless an egg is perfectly good, it is unfit for any purpose whatever, and will spoil whatever it is mixed with. You may judge with tolerable accuracy of the state of an egg by holding it against the sun or the candle, and if the yolk, as you see it through the shell, appears round, and the white thin and clear, it is most probably a good one; but if the yolk looks broken, and the white thick and cloudy, the egg is certainly bad. You may try the freshness of eggs by putting them into a pan of cold water. Those that sink the soonest are the freshest; those that are stale or addled will float on the surface.

There are various ways of preserving eggs. To keep them merely for plain boiling, you may parboil them for one minute, and then bury them in powdered charcoal with their small ends downward. They will keep a few days in a jar of salt; but do not afterwards use the salt in which they have been immersed.

They are frequently preserved for two or three months by greasing them all over, when quite fresh, with melted mutton suet, and then wedging them close together (the small end downwards) in a box of bran, layer above layer; the box must be closely covered.

Another way (and a very good one) is to put some lime in a large vessel, and slack it with boiling water, till it is of the consistence of thin cream; you may allow a gallon of water to a pound of lime. When it is cold, pour it off into a large stone jar, put in the eggs, and cover the jar closely. See that the eggs are always well covered with the lime-water, and lest they should break, avoid moving the jar. If you have hens of your own, keep a jar of lime-water always ready, and put in the eggs as they are brought in from the nests. Jars that hold about six quarts are the most convenient.

It will be well to renew the lime-water occasionally.

TO BOIL EGGS FOR BREAKFAST.

The fresher they are the longer time they will require for boiling. If you wish them quite soft, put them into a sauce-pan of water that is boiling hard at the moment, and let them remain in it five minutes. The longer they boil the harder they will be. In ten minutes' fast boiling they will be hard enough for salad.

If you use one of the tin egg-boilers that are placed on the table, see that the water is boiling hard at the time you put in the eggs. When they have been in about four or five minutes, take them out, pour off the water, and replace it by some more that is boiling hard; as, from the coldness of the eggs having chilled the first water, they will not otherwise be done enough. The boiler may then be placed on the table, (keeping the lid closed,) and in a few minutes more they will be sufficiently cooked to be wholesome.

TO POACH EGGS.

Pour some boiling water out of a tea kettle through a clean cloth spread over the top of a broad stew-pan; for by observing this process the eggs will be nicer and more easily done than when its impurities remain in the water. Set the pan with the strained water on hot coals, and when it boils break each egg separately into a saucer. Remove the pan from the fire, and slip the eggs one by one into the surface of the water. Let the pan stand till the white of the eggs is set; then place it again on the coals, and as soon as the water boils again, the eggs will be sufficiently done. Take them out carefully with an egg-slice, and trim off all the ragged edges from the white, which should thinly cover the yolk. Have ready some thin slices of buttered toast with the crust cut off. Lay them in the bottom of the dish, with a poached egg on each slice of toast, and send them to the breakfast table.

FRICASSEED EGGS.

Take a dozen eggs, and boil them six or seven minutes, or till they are just hard enough to peel and slice without breaking. Then put them into a pan of cold water while you prepare some grated bread-crumbs, (seasoned with pepper, salt and nutmeg,) and beat the yolks of two or three raw eggs very light. Take the boiled eggs out of the water, and having peeled off the shells, slice the eggs, dust a little flour over them, and dip them first into the beaten egg, and then into the bread-crumbs so as to cover them well on both sides. Have ready in a frying-pan some boiling lard; put the sliced eggs into it, and fry them on both sides. Serve them up at the breakfast table, garnished with small sprigs of parsley that has been fried in the same lard after the eggs were taken out.

PLAIN OMELET.

Take six eggs, leaving out the whites of two. Beat them very light, and strain them through a sieve. Add pepper and salt to your taste. Divide two ounces of fresh butter into little bits, and put it into the egg. Have ready a quarter of a pound of butter in a frying-pan, or a flat stew-pan. Place it on hot coals, and have the butter boiling when you put in the beaten egg. Fry it gently till of a light brown on the under side. Do not turn it while cooking as it will do better without. You may brown the top by holding a hot shovel over it. When done, lay it in the dish, double it in half, and stick sprigs of curled parsley over it.

You may flavour the omelet by mixing with the beaten egg some parsley or sweet herbs minced fine, some chopped celery, or chopped onion, allowing two moderate sized onions to an omelet of six eggs. Or what is still better, it may be seasoned with veal kidney or sweet-bread minced; with cold ham shred as fine as possible; or with minced oysters, (the hard part omitted,) with tops of asparagus (that has been previously boiled) cut into small pieces.

You should have one of the pans that are made purposely for omelets.

AN OMELETTE SOUFFLÉ.

Break eight eggs, separate the whites from the yolks, and strain them. Put the whites into one pan, and the yolks into another, and beat them separately with rods till the yolks are very thick and smooth, and the whites a stiff froth that will stand alone. Then add gradually to the yolks, three quarters of a pound of the finest powdered loaf-sugar, and orange-flower water or lemon-juice to your taste. Next stir the whites lightly into the yolks. Butter a deep pan or dish (that has been previously heated) and pour the mixture rapidly into it. Set it in a Butch oven with coals under it, and on the top, and bake it five minutes. If properly beaten and mixed, and carefully baked, it will rise very high. Send it immediately to table, or it will fall and flatten.

Do not begin to make an omelette soufflé till the company at table have commenced their dinner, that it may be ready to serve up just in time, immediately on the removal of the meats. The whole must be accomplished as quickly as possible, and it must be cut and sent round directly that it is brought to table.

If you live in a large town, the safest way of avoiding a failure in an omelette soufflé is to hire a French cook to come to your kitchen with his own utensils and ingredients, and make and bake it himself, while the first part of the dinner is progressing in the dining room.

An omelette soufflé is a very nice and delicate thing when properly managed; but if flat and heavy it should not be brought to table.

TO DRESS MACCARONI.

Have ready a pot of boiling water. Throw a little salt into it, and then by slow degrees put in a pound of the maccaroni, a little at a time. Keep stirring it gently, and continue to do so very often while boiling. Take care to keep it well covered with water. Have ready a kettle of boiling water to replenish the maccaroni pot if it should be in danger of getting too dry. In about twenty minutes it will be done. It must be quite soft, but it must not boil long enough to break.

When the maccaroni has boiled sufficiently, pour in immediately a little cold water, and let it stand a few minutes, keeping it covered.

Grate half a pound of Parmesan cheese into a deep dish, and scatter over it a few small bits of butter. Then with a skimmer that is perforated with holes, commence taking up the maccaroni, (draining it well,) and spread a layer of it over the cheese and butter. Spread over it another layer of grated cheese and butter, and then a layer of maccaroni and so on till your dish is full; having a layer of maccaroni on the top, over which spread some butter without cheese. Cover the dish, and set it in an oven for half an hour. It will then be ready to send to table.

You may grate some nutmeg over each, layer of maccaroni.

PICKLING

GENERAL REMARKS.

Never on any consideration use brass, copper, or bell-metal settles for pickling; the verdigris produced in them by the vinegar being of a most poisonous nature. Kettles lined with porcelain are the best, but if you cannot procure them, block tin may be substituted. Iron is apt to discolour any acid that is boiled in it.

Vinegar for pickles should always be of the very best kind. In putting away pickles, use stone, or glass jars. The lead which is an ingredient in the glazing of common earthenware, is rendered very pernicious by the action of the vinegar. Have a large wooden spoon and a fork, for the express purpose of taking pickles out of the jar when you want them for the table. See that, while in the jar, they are always completely covered with vinegar. If you discern in them any symptoms of not keeping well, do them over again in fresh vinegar and spice.

Vinegar for pickles should only boil five or six minutes.

The jars should be stopped with large flat corks, fitting closely, and having a leather or a round piece of oil-cloth tied over the cork.

It is a good rule to have two-thirds of the jar filled with pickles, and one-third with vinegar.

Alum is very useful in extracting the salt taste from pickles, and in making them firm and crisp. A very small quantity is sufficient. Too much will spoil them.

In greening pickles keep them very closely covered, so that none of the steam may escape; as its retention promotes their greenness and prevents the flavour from evaporating.

Vinegar and spice for pickles should be boiled but a few minutes. Too much boiling takes away the strength.

TO PICKLE CUCUMBERS.

Cucumbers for pickling should be very small, and as free from spots as possible. Make a brine of salt and water strong enough to bear an egg. Pour it over your cucumbers, cover them with fresh cabbage leaves, and let them stand for a week, or till they are quite yellow, stirring them at least twice a day. When they are perfectly yellow, pour off the water. Take a porcelain kettle, and cover the bottom and sides with fresh vine leaves. Put in the cucumbers (with a small piece of alum) and cover them closely with vine leaves all over the top, and then with a dish or cloth to keep in the steam. Fill up the kettle with clear water, and hang it over the fire when dinner is done, but not where there is a blaze. The fire under the kettle must be kept very moderate. The water must not boil, or be too hot to bear your hand in. Keep them over the fire in a slow heat till next morning. If they are not then of a fine green, repeat the process. When they are well greened, take them out of the kettle, drain them on a sieve, and put them into a clean stone jar. Boil for five or six minutes sufficient of the best vinegar to cover the cucumbers well; putting into the kettle a thin muslin bag filled with cloves, mace, and mustard seed. Pour the vinegar scalding hot into the jar of pickles, which should be secured with a large flat cork, and an oil-cloth or leather cover tied over it. Another way to green pickles is to cover them with vine leaves or cabbage leaves, and to keep them on a warm, hearth pouring boiling water on them five or six times a day; renewing the water as soon as it becomes cold.

In proportioning the spice to the vinegar, allow to every two quarts, an ounce of mace, two dozen cloves, and two ounces of mustard seed. You may leave the muslin bag, with the spice, for about a week in the pickle jar to heighten the flavour, if you think it necessary.

GREEN PEPPERS.

May be done in the same manner as cucumbers, only extracting the seeds before you put the pickles into the salt and water. Do not put peppers into the same jar with cucumbers, as the former will destroy the latter.

GHERKINS.

The gherkin is a small thick oval-shaped species of cucumber with a hairy or prickly surface, and is cultivated solely for pickling. It is customary to let the stems remain on them. Wipe them dry, put them into a broad stone jar, and scald them five or six times in the course of the day with salt and water strong enough to bear an egg, and let them set all night. This will make them yellow. Next day, having drained them from the salt and water, throw it out, wipe them dry, put them into a clean vessel (with a little piece of alum,) and scald them with boiling vinegar and water, (half and half of each,) repeating it frequently during the day till they are green. Keep them as closely covered as possible. Then put them away in stone jars, mixing among them whole mace and sliced ginger to your taste. Fill up with cold vinegar, and add a little alum, allowing to every hundred gherkins a piece about the size of a shelled almond. The alum will make them firm and crisp.

RADISH PODS.

Gather sprigs or bunches of radish pods while they are young and tender, but let the pods remain on the sprigs; it not being the custom to pick them off. Put them into strong salt and water, and let them stand two days. Then drain and wipe them and put them into a clean stone jar. Boil an equal quantity of vinegar and water. Pour it over the radish pods while hot, and cover them closely to keep in the steam. Repeat this frequently through the day till they are very green. Then pour off the vinegar and water, and boil for five minutes some very strong vinegar, with a little bit of alum, and pour it over them. Put them into a stone jar, (and having added some whole mace, whole pepper, a little tumeric and a little sweet oil,) cork it closely, and tie over it a leather or oil-cloth.

GREEN BEANS.

Take young green or French beans; string them, but do not cut them in pieces. Pat them in salt and water for two days, stirring them frequently. Then put them into a kettle with vine or cabbage leaves under, over, and all round them, (adding a little piece of alum.) Cover them closely to keep in the steam, and let them hang over a slow fire till they are a fine green.

Having drained them in a sieve, make for them a pickle of strong vinegar, and boil in it for five minutes, some mace, whole pepper, and sliced ginger tied up in a thin muslin bag. Pour it hot upon the beans, put them into a stone jar, and tie them up.

PARSLEY.

Make a brine of salt and water strong enough to bear an egg, and throw into it a large quantity of curled parsley, tied up in little bunches with a thread. After it has stood a week (stirring it several times a day) take it out, drain it well, and lay it for three days in cold spring or pump-water, changing the water daily. Then scald it in hard water, and hang it, well covered, over a slow fire till it becomes green. Afterwards take it out, and drain and press it till quite dry.

Boil for five minutes a quart of strong vinegar with a small bit of alum, a few blades of mace, a sliced nutmeg, and a few slips of horseradish. Pour it on the parsley, and put it away in a stone jar.

MANGOES.

Take very young oval shaped musk-melons. Cut a round piece out of the top or side of each, (saving the piece to put on again,) and extract the seeds. Then (having tied on the pieces with packthread) put them into strong salt and water for two days. Afterwards drain and wipe them, put them into a kettle with vine leaves or cabbage leaves under and over them, and a little piece of alum, and hang them on a slow fire to green; keeping them closely covered to retain the steam, which will greatly accelerate the greening. When they are quite green, have ready the stuffing, which must be a mixture of scraped horseradish, white mustard seed, mace and nutmeg pounded, race ginger cut small, pepper, tumeric and sweet oil. Fill your mangoes with this mixture, putting a small clove of garlic into each, and replacing the pieces at the openings; tie them with a packthread crossing backwards and forwards round the mango. Put them into stone jars, pour boiling vinegar over them, and cover them well. Before you put them on the table remove the packthread.

NASTURTIANS.

Have ready a stone or glass jar of the best cold vinegar. Take the green seeds of the nasturtian after the flower has gone off. They should be full-grown but not old. Pick off the stems, and put the seeds into the vinegar. No other preparation is necessary, and they will keep a year with nothing more than sufficient cold vinegar to cover them. With boiled mutton they are an excellent substitute for capers.

MORELLA CHERRIES.

See that all your cherries are perfect. Remove the stems, and put the cherries into a jar or glass with sufficient vinegar to cover them well. They will keep perfectly in a cool dry place.

They are very good, always retaining the taste of the cherry. If you cannot procure morellas, the large red pie-cherries may be substituted.

PEACHES.

Take, fine large peaches (either cling or free stones) that are not too ripe. Wipe off the down with a clean flannel, and put the peaches whole into a stone jar. Cover them with cold vinegar of the best kind, in which you have dissolved a little of salt, allowing a table-spoonful to a quart of vinegar. Put a cork in the jar and tie leather or oil-cloth over it.

Plums and grapes may be pickled thus in cold vinegar, but without salt.

BARBERRIES.

Have ready a jar of cold vinegar, and put into it ripe barberries in bunches. They make a pretty garnish for the edges of dishes.

TO PICKLE GREEN PEPPERS.

The bell pepper is the best for pickling, and should be gathered when quite young. Slit one side, and carefully take out the core, so as not to injure the shell of the pepper. Then put them into boiling salt and water, changing the water every day for one week, and keeping them closely covered in a warm place near the fire. Stir them several times a day. They will first become yellow, and then green. When they are a fine green put them into a jar, and pour cold vinegar over them, adding a small piece of alum.

They require no spice.

You may stuff the peppers as you do mangoes.

TO PICKLE BUTTERNUTS.

These nuts are in the best state for pickling when the shell is soft, and when they are so young that the outer skin can be penetrated by the head of a pin. They should be gathered when the sun is hot upon them.

If you have a large quantity, the easiest way to prepare them for pickling is to put them into a tub with sufficient lye to cover them, and to stir and rub them about with a hickory broom, till they are clean and smooth on the outside. This is much less trouble than scraping them, and is not so likely to injure the nuts. Another method is to scald them, and then to rub off the outer skin. Put the nuts into strong salt and water for nine or ten days; changing the water every other day, and keeping them closely covered from the air. Then drain and wipe them, (piercing each nut through in several places with a large needle,) and prepare the pickle as follows:—For a hundred large nuts, take of black pepper and ginger root of each an ounce; and of cloves, mace and nutmeg of each a half ounce. Pound all the spices to powder, and mix them well together, adding two large spoonfuls of mustard seed. Put the nuts into jars, (having first stuck each of them through in several places with a large needle,) strewing the powdered seasoning between every layer of nuts. Boil for five minutes a gallon of the best white wine vinegar, and pour it boiling hot upon the nuts. Secure the jars closely with corks and leathers. You may begin to eat the nuts in a fortnight.

Walnuts may be pickled in the same manner.

TO PICKLE WALNUTS BLACK.

The walnuts should he gathered while young and soft, (so that you can easily run a pin through them,) and when the sun is upon them. Rub them with a coarse flannel or tow cloth to get off the fur of the outside. Mix salt and water strong enough to bear an egg, and let them lie in it nine days, (changing it every two days,) and stirring them, frequently. Then take them out, drain them, spread them on large dishes, and expose them to the air about ten minutes, which will cause them to blacken the sooner. Scald them in boiling water, (but do not let them lie in it,) and then rub them with a coarse woollen cloth, and pierce everyone through in several places with a large needle, (that the pickle may penetrate them thoroughly.) Put them into stone jars, and prepare the spice and vinegar. To a hundred walnuts allow a gallon of vinegar, an ounce of cloves, an ounce of allspice, an ounce of black pepper, half an ounce of mace, and half an ounce of nutmeg. Boil the spice in the vinegar for five or six minutes; then, strain the vinegar, and pour it boiling hot over the walnuts. Tie up in a thin muslin rag, a tea-cupful of mustard seed, and a large table-spoonful of scraped horseradish, and put it into the jars with the walnuts. Cover them closely with corks and leathers.

Another way of pickling walnuts black, is (after preparing them as above) to put them into jars with the spices pounded and strewed among them, and then to pour over them strong cold vinegar.

WALNUTS PICKLED WHITE.

Take large young walnuts while their shells are quite soft so that you can stick the head of a pin into them. Pare them very thin till the white appears; and as you do them, throw them into spring or pump water in which some salt has been dissolved. Let them stand in that water six hours, with a thin board upon them to keep them down under the water. Fill a porcelain kettle with fresh spring water, and set it over a clear fire, or on a charcoal furnace. Put the walnuts into the kettle, cover it, and let them simmer (but not boil) for five or six minutes. Then have ready a vessel with cold spring water and salt, and put your nuts into it, taking them out of the kettle with a wooden ladle. Let them stand in the cold salt and water for a quarter of an hour, with the board keeping them down as before; for if they rise above the liquor, or are exposed to the air, they will be discoloured. Then take, them out, and lay them on a cloth covered with another, till they are quite dry. Afterwards rub them carefully with a soft flannel, and put them into a stone jar; laying among them blades of mace, and sliced nutmeg, but no dark-coloured spice. Pour over them the best distilled vinegar, and put on the top a table-spoonful of sweet oil.

WALNUTS PICKLED GREEN.

Gather them while the shells are very soft, and rub them all with a flannel. Then wrap them singly in vine leaves, lay a few vine leaves in the bottom of a large stone jar, put in the walnuts, (seeing that each of them is well wrapped up so as not to touch one another,) and cover them with a thick layer of leaves. Fill up the jar with strong vinegar, cover it closely, and let it stand three weeks. Then pour off the vinegar, take out the walnuts, renew all the vine leaves, fill up with fresh vinegar, and let them stand three weeks longer. Then again pour off the vinegar, and renew the vine leaves. This time take the best white wine vinegar; put salt in it till it will bear an egg, and add to it mace, sliced nutmeg, and scraped horseradish, in the proportion of an ounce of each and a gallon of vinegar to a hundred walnuts. Boil the spice and vinegar about eight minutes, and then pour it hot on the walnuts. Cover the jar closely with a cork and leather, and set it away, leaving the vine leaves with the walnuts. When you take any out for use, disturb the others as little as possible, and do not put back again any that may be left.

You may pickle butternuts green in the same manner.

TO PICKLE ONIONS.

Take very small onions, and with a sharp knife cut off the stems as close as possible, and peel off the outer skin. Then put them into salt and water, and let them stand in the brine for six days; stirring them daily, and changing the salt and water every two days. See that they are closely covered. Then put the onions into jars, and give them a scald in boiling salt and water. Let them stand till they are cold; then drain them on a sieve, wipe them, stick a clove in the top of each and put them into wide-mouthed bottles; dispersing among them some blades of mace and slices of ginger or nutmeg. Fill up the bottles with the best white wine vinegar, and put at the top a large spoonful of salad oil. Cork the bottles well.

ONIONS PICKLED WHITE.

Peel some very small white onions, and lay them for three days in salt and water changing the water every day. Then wipe them, and put them into a porcelain kettle with equal quantities of milk and water, sufficient to cover them well. Simmer them over a slow fire, but when just ready to boil take them off, and drain and dry them, and put them into wide-mouthed glass bottles; interspersing them with blades of mace. Boil a sufficient quantity of distilled white wine vinegar to cover them and fill up the bottles, adding to it a little salt; and when it is cold, pour it into the bottles of onions. At the top of each bottle put a spoonful of sweet oil. Set them away closely corked.

TO PICKLE MUSHROOMS WHITE.

Take small fresh-gathered button mushrooms, peel them carefully with a penknife, and cut off the stems; throwing the mushrooms into salt and water as you do them. Then put them into a porcelain skillet of fresh water, cover it closely, and set it over a quick fire. Boil it as fast as possible for seven or eight minutes, not more. Take out the mushrooms, drain them, and spread them on a clean board, with the bottom or hollow side of each mushroom turned downwards. Do this as quickly as possible, and immediately, while they are hot, sprinkle them over with salt. When they are cold, put them into a glass jar with slight layers of mace and sliced ginger. Fill up the jar with cold distilled or white wine vinegar. Put a spoonful of sweet oil on the top of each jar, and cork it closely.

MUSHROOMS PICKLED BROWN.

Take a quart of large mushrooms and (having trimmed off the stalks) rub them with a flannel cloth dipped in salt. Then lay them in a pan of allegar or ale vinegar, for a quarter of an hour, and wash them about in it. Then pat them into a sauce-pan with a quart of allegar, a quarter of an ounce of cloves, the same of allspice and whole pepper, and a tea-spoonful of salt. Set the pan over coals, and let the mushrooms stew slowly for ten minutes, keeping the pan well covered. Then take them off, let them get cold by degrees, and put them into small bottles with the allegar strained from the spice and poured upon them.

It will be prudent to boil an onion with the mushrooms, and if it turns black or blueish, you may infer that there is a poisonous one among them; and they should therefore be thrown away. Stir them for the same reason, with a silver spoon.

TO PICKLE TOMATAS.

Take a peck of tomatas, (the small round ones are best for pickling,) and prick every one with a fork. Put them into a broad stone or earthen vessel, and sprinkle salt between every layer of tomatas. Cover them, and let them remain three days in the salt. Then put them into vinegar and water mixed in equal quantities, half and half, and keep them in it twenty-four hours to draw out the saltness. There must be sufficient of the liquid to cover the tomatas well.

To a peck of tomatas allow a bottle of mustard, half an ounce of cloves, and half an ounce of pepper, with a dozen onions sliced thin. Pack the tomatas in a stone jar, placing the spices and onions alternately with the layers of tomatas. Put them in till the jar is two-thirds fall. Then fill it up with strong cold vinegar, and stop it closely. The pickles will be fit to eat in a fortnight.

If you do not like onions, substitute for them a larger quantity of spice.

TOMATA SOY.

For this purpose you must have the best and ripest tomatas, and they must be gathered on a dry day. Do not peel them, but merely cut them into slices. Having strewed some salt over the bottom of a tub, put in the tomatas in layers; sprinkling between each layer (which, should be about two inches in thickness) a half pint of salt. Repeat this till you have put in eight quarts or one peck of tomatas. Cover the tub and let it set for three days. Then early in the morning, put the tomatas into a large porcelain, kettle, and boil it slowly and steadily till ten at night, frequently mashing and stirring the tomatas. Then put it out to cool. Next morning strain and press it through a sieve, and when no more liquid will pass through, put it into a clean kettle with two ounces of cloves, one ounce of mace, two ounces of blade pepper, and two table-spoonfuls of cayenne, all powdered.

Again let it boil slowly and steadily all day, and put it to cool in the evening in a large pan. Cover it, and let it set all night. Next day put it into small bottles, securing the corks by dipping them in melted rosin, and tying leathers over them.

If made exactly according to these directions, and slowly and thoroughly boiled, it will keep for years in a cool dry place, and may be used for many purposes when fresh tomatas are not to be had.

TO PICKLE CAULIFLOWERS.

Take the whitest and closest full-grown cauliflowers; cut off the thick stalk, and split the blossom or flower part into eight or ten pieces. Spread them oh a large dish, sprinkle them with salt, and let them stand twenty-four hours. Then wash off the salt, drain them, put them into a broad flat jar or pan, scald them with salt and water, (allowing a quarter of a pound of salt to a quart of water,) cover them closely and let them stand in the brine till next day. Afterwards drain them in a hair sieve, and spread them on a cloth in a warm place to dry for a day and a night. Then put them carefully, piece by piece, into clean broad jars and pour over them a pickle which has been prepared as follows:—Mix together three ounces of coriander seed, three ounces of turmeric, one ounce of mustard seed, and one ounce of ginger. Pound the whole in a mortar to a fine powder. Put it into three quarts of the best white wine vinegar, set it by the side of the fire in a stone jar, and let it infuse three days. These are the proportions, but the quantity of the whole pickle must depend on the quantity of cauliflower, which must he kept well covered by the liquid. Pour it over the cauliflower, and secure the jars closely from the air.

You may pickle brocoli in the same manner. Also the green tops of asparagus.

TO PICKLE RED CABBAGE.

Take a fine firm cabbage of a deep red or purple colour. Strip off the outer leaves, and cut out the stalk. Quarter the cabbage lengthways, and then slice it crossways. Lay it in a deep dish, sprinkle a handful of salt over it, cover it with another dish, and let it lie twenty-four hours. Then drain it in a cullender from the salt, and wipe it dry. Make a pickle of sufficient white wine vinegar to cover the cabbage well, adding to it equal quantities of cloves and allspice, with some mace. The spices must be put in whole, with a little cochineal to give it a good red colour. Boil the vinegar and spices hard for five minutes, and having put the cabbage into a stone jar, pour the vinegar over it boiling hot. Cover the jar with a cloth till it gets cold; and then put in a large cork, and tie a leather over it.

COLD SLAW.

[Footnote: This receipt was accidentally omitted in its proper place.]

Take a nice fresh cabbage, wash and drain it, and cut off all the stalk. Shave down the head into very small slips, with a cabbage cutter, or a very sharp knife. It must be done evenly and nicely. Put it into a deep china dish, and prepare for it the following dressing. Melt in a sauce-pan a quarter of a pound of butter, with half a pint of water, a large table-spoonful of vinegar, a salt-spoon of salt, and a little cayenne. Give this a boil up, and pour it hot upon the cabbage.

Send it to table as soon as it is cold.

WARM SLAW.

Cut the cabbage into shavings as for cold slaw; (red cabbage is best;) and put it into a deep earthen dish. Cover it closely, and set it on the top of a stove, or in a slack oven for half an hour till it is warm all through; but do not let it get so heated as to boil. Then make a mixture as for cold slaw, of a quarter of a pound of butter, half a pint of water, a little salt and cayenne, and add to it a clove of garlic minced fine. Boil this mixture in a sauce-pan, and pour it hot over the warm cabbage. Send it to table immediately.

This is a French method of dressing cabbage.

EAST INDIA PICKLE.

This is a mixture of various things pickled together, and put into the same jar.

Have ready a small white cabbage, sliced, and the stalk removed; a cauliflower cut into neat branches, leaving out the large stalk; sliced cucumbers; sliced carrots; sliced beets, (all nicked round the edges;) button-onions; string-beans; radish pods; barberries; cherries; green grapes; nasturtians; capsicums; bell-peppers, &c. Sprinkle all these things with salt, put them promiscuously into a large earthen pan, and pour scalding salt and water over them. Let them lie in the brine for four days, turning them all over every day. Then take them out, wash each thing separately in vinegar, and wipe them carefully in a cloth. Afterwards lay them on sieves before the fire and dry them thoroughly.

For the pickle liquor.—To every two quarts of the best vinegar, put an ounce and a half of white ginger root, scraped and sliced; the same of long pepper; two ounces of peeled shalots, or little button-onions, cut in pieces; half an ounce of peeled garlic; an ounce of-turmeric; and two ounces of mustard seed bruised, or of mustard powder. Let all these ingredients, mixed with the vinegar, infuse in a close jar for a week, setting in a warm place, or by the fire. Then (after the vegetables have been properly prepared, and dried from the brine) put them all into one large stone jar, or into smaller jars, and strain the pickle over them. The liquid must be in a large quantity, so as to keep the vegetables well covered with it, or they will spoil. Put a table-spoonful of sweet oil on the top of each jar, and secure them well with a large cork and a leather.

If you find that after awhile the vegetables have absorbed the liquor, so that there is danger of their not having a sufficiency, prepare some more seasoned vinegar and pour it over them.

East India pickle is very convenient, and will keep two years. As different vegetables come into season, you can prepare them with the salt and water process, and add them to the things already in the jar. You may put small mangoes into this pickle; also plums, peaches and apricots.

TO PICKLE OYSTERS FOR KEEPING.

For this purpose take none but the finest and largest oysters. After they are opened, separate them from their liquor, and put them into a bucket or a large pan, and pour boiling water upon them to take out the slime. Stir them about in it, and then take them out, and rinse them well in cold water. Then put them into a large kettle with fresh water, barely enough to cover them, (mixing with it a table-spoonful of salt to every hundred oysters,) and give them a boil up, just sufficient to plump them. Take them, out, spread them on large dishes or on a clean table, and cover them with a cloth. Take the liquor of the oysters, and with every pint of it mix a quart of the best vinegar, a table-spoonful of salt, a table-spoonful of whole cloves, the same of whole black pepper, and a tea-spoonful of whole mace. Put the liquid over the fire in a kettle, and when it boils throw in the oysters, and let them remain in it five minutes. Then take the whole off the fire, stir it up well, and let it stand to get quite cold. Afterwards (if you have a large quantity) put it into a keg, which must first be well scalded, (a new keg is best,) and fill it as full as it can hold. Do not put a weight on the oysters to keep them down in the liquor, as it will crush them to pieces if the keg should be moved or conveyed to a distance. If you have not enough to fill a keg, put them into stone jars when they are perfectly cold, and cover them securely.

www.ingramcontent.com/pod-product-compliance
Lightning Source LLC
Chambersburg PA
CBHW081112080526
44587CB00021B/3561